Autism in the Early Years

A Practical Guide

Val Cumine, Julia Leach and Gill Stevenson

David Fulton Publishers
London

David Fulton Publishers Ltd
Ormond House, 26–27 Boswell Street, London WC1N 3JZ
www.fultonpublishers.co.uk

First published in Great Britain in 2000 by David Fulton Publishers
Reprinted 2000

Note: The right of Val Cumine, Julia Leach and Gill Stevenson to be identified as the authors of this work has been asserted by them in accordance with the Copyright, Designs and Patents Act 1988.

British Library Cataloguing in Publication Data
A catalogue record for this book is available from the British Library

ISBN 1–85346–599–2

Typeset by Textype Typesetters, Cambridge
Printed in Great Britain by Bell and Bain Ltd, Glasgow

Contents

Preface

This book stems, in the first instance, from the authors' joint involvement in a three-year autism research project in Lancashire. During that three-year period the authors met around 200 children with autistic spectrum disorders in a variety of settings.

In their present professional roles, the authors continue to have direct involvement with young children with autism and their families. The content of the book draws on this breadth of experience. The anecdotes in the book are all based on real children, but names have been changed to protect confidentiality.

The authors have used the convention of referring to children as 'he' and teachers/practitioners as 'she' throughout.

Figure 0.1 James prefers to sit at the edge of the group

Val Cumine, Julia Leach and Gill Stevenson
Lancashire
August 2000

1 Autism: an introduction

Purpose of the book

This book sets out to provide parents and professionals with an insight into the nature and educational implications of autism, particularly as it presents in very young children. Consideration will be given to the issues surrounding assessment and diagnosis.

In addition, the book aims to equip Early Years practitioners and parents with knowledge of a range of intervention strategies to promote learning, social development, communication and appropriate behaviour. The book goes on to explore the possibilities for enhancing access to the Early Years curriculum.

History

There is no doubt that there have been people with autism throughout history. However it was not until the 1930s that the first systematic study of autism took place in Boston, USA. Leo Kanner reported the findings of this study in 1943 in his paper 'Autistic disturbance of affective contact'.

Kanner was a pioneer in the field of child psychiatry. His study began in 1938 when a fascinating five year old, Donald, was brought to his clinic. From the age of two and a half, Donald had been able to list the names of all the US Presidents, say the alphabet backwards and forwards, and recite the 23rd Psalm – although he was unable to carry on a normal conversation. Over the next few years, Kanner saw ten more children who displayed similar behaviour patterns. Their parents commented they were 'self-sufficient', 'like a shell', 'happiest when left alone', 'acting as if people weren't there', 'giving the impression of silent wisdom'.

Kanner's paper was circulated, discussed and reviewed within the psychiatric world and considered an important breakthrough in the understanding of children who up to this time had appeared beyond help. Kanner used the term 'early childhood autism' which he may have felt emphasised both the time of the first manifestations of the disorder and the child's limited accessibility.

For Kanner the defining features of autism were:

- a profound autistic withdrawal;
- an obsessive desire for the preservation of sameness;
- a good rote memory;
- an intelligent and pensive expression;
- mutism, or language without real communicative intent;
- over-sensitivity to stimuli;
- a skilful relationship to objects.

Kanner explained that he referred to the work of Bleuler (1911) when choosing the word 'autism' to describe what he saw. Bleuler used the term to describe a withdrawal from previous participation, whereas the children Kanner described had never engaged in social interaction.

Triad of impairments

As the information provided by Kanner's observations on the nature of autism became more widely known, more children were referred for diagnosis. Sets of criteria and checklists were developed to aid diagnosis. As more children were seen, it became clear that Kanner had only recognised one small group of children who fitted his particular criteria. The list of Kanner's defining features was felt to be too limiting by those who were involved in diagnosis. There were children for whom it was felt that a diagnosis of autism would be a useful descriptor yet who did not fit exactly into the criteria outlined by Kanner.

In 1979 Lorna Wing and Judith Gould carried out a study in the London Borough of Camberwell, looking at all children under 15 who had any kind of physical or learning disability or abnormality of behaviour, however mild or severe. Examining the findings of their study they were able to pinpoint the social nature of the difficulties and identified what they described as the 'Autism Triad' of impairments:

- impairment of social interaction;
- impairment of social communication;
- impairment of social imagination.

Autistic spectrum

Wing and Gould identified a number of children with what they described as 'Kanner's syndrome', and a larger number who showed similarities to this group, but didn't fit Kanner's criteria exactly. Thus, in 1988 Wing went on to use the broader term 'Autistic Continuum' and later 'Autistic Spectrum' (Wing 1996).

The term 'spectrum' has been useful in allowing for a broad definition of autism based on the Triad of Impairments and has been described as being most appropriate in facilitating educational approaches to autism by Jordan (1999). Intervention and treatment approaches for children anywhere within the autistic spectrum will share the same foundation.

Diagnostic criteria

Diagnosis of autism continues to be based on the interpretation of a child's observed and reported behaviours – not the most clear-cut diagnostic tool. Although it is recognised that autism can occur whatever the intellectual capacity, many of the children may also have an additional general learning difficulty. This adds to the difficulty in diagnosis, as it becomes increasingly difficult to separate out the effects of autism and the effects of profound and multiple difficulties.

Wing and Gould (1979) in the Camberwell study found that 60 per cent of the children with autism had Severe Learning Difficulties, 25 per cent had Moderate Learning Difficulties and 15 per cent were of average and above average intelligence.

There is acceptance now that autism is distinguished by the co-occurrence of the impairments in social interaction, social communication, social imagination, flexible thinking and play. Diagnostic criteria are agreed on the basis of the triad. The two major diagnostic instruments currently used by clinicians base their criteria on these three fundamental impairments, i.e. DSM IV (*Diagnostic and Statistical Manual of Mental Disorders*, 4th edition, American Psychiatric Association (APA) 1994) and ICD 10 (*International Classification of Diseases*, World Health Organisation (WHO) 1992).

Numbers of children

There have been attempts to define the number of people with autism; the totals identified ranging from 5 per 10,000 population to 91 per 10,000. This wide range of prevalence figures causes confusion if it is not looked at with care. Most studies suggest between 4 and 6 per 10,000 who can be classified as having 'Kanner's autism'. The National Autistic Society (1997) suggests a prevalence figure of 91 per 10,000. This figure relates to the broadest definition of autism, including those with classic 'Kanner's autism', those who may best be described as having Asperger syndrome, together with those who have impairments within the triad, but do not fit into either Kanner's autism or Asperger syndrome.

All prevalence studies reflect Kanner's findings that boys outnumber girls in the autistic community. Ciadella and Mamelle (1989) suggest two boys to every one girl, while Lord and Schopler (1987) suggest the ratio is 5:1.

Causes

As yet the cause of autism is unknown. It is felt that there is not one single cause, rather a set of triggers any one of which, if it occurs at a certain time within a chain of circumstances, can cause autism (see Figure 1.1).

In 1991 Uta Frith described autism as, 'a developmental disorder due to a specific brain abnormality with its origins in genetic fault, brain insult or brain disease'. Researchers are looking at the areas of the brain in which dysfunction may occur. As technology continues to improve it may be possible to give a precise indication of the location of areas of dysfunction.

Until there is more information as to the causes of autism and the possible interventions at a very early stage it may be more useful to specify the functions lost or impaired and look for ways in which intervention may help at this stage.

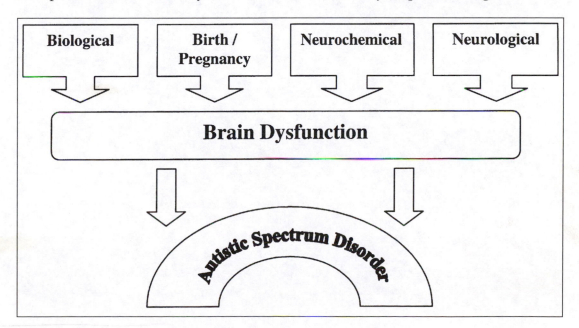

Figure 1.1 Factors which may trigger autistic spectrum disorders

Summary

- Child psychiatrist, Leo Kanner, first described autism in 1943.
- Autism is regarded as a physical disorder of the brain which causes a lifelong developmental disability.
- Estimates of the prevalence of autism range from 5 per 10,000 of population to 91 per 10,000.
- Boys are more likely to be affected than girls – with suggested ratios ranging from 2:1 to 13:1.
- Autism affects children right across the ability range.

2 Assessment and diagnosis

Key features of autism

Autism is characterised by significant impairments in three areas of development. Typical features which present in the Early Years include the following:

1. Social interaction

The young child with autism:

- Cannot make sense of people, and may find them frighteningly unpredictable.
- Seems to relate better to objects than to people.
- May only tolerate approaches from very familiar people.
- May only make approaches to people he knows well.
- May seem to use people only as a means to an end – perhaps to obtain something out of their own reach. (Richard preferred to help himself to food from the kitchen, dragging a chair to help him climb up and open the cupboard. Only if this strategy failed would he pull his Mum into the kitchen and 'throw' her hand up towards the item he wanted – all without vocalisation or eye contact.)
- Is usually unaware of simple social rules and conventions.

2. Social communication

The young child with autism:

- Is slow to develop speech – and may not develop speech at all.
- If he uses words, often uses them out of context and without communicative intent.
- May echo the words of others – straight away, or later. (Curtis spoke with an American accent, despite having English parents – he'd acquired most of his language from repeatedly watching cartoon videos.)
- May use words and then 'lose' them. (At 18 months Lewis was shouting 'Daddy' up the stairs, and had around 20 words in his vocabulary. By the age of two he was mostly silent.)
- Uses little communicative eye gaze.
- Rarely understands or uses gesture.
- May develop a pointing gesture, but use it to indicate need rather than to share an experience.

3. Social imagination and flexibility of thought

The young child with autism:

- Cannot easily make sense of sequences of events. (Mark used to enter the playroom with a frown, and then would stand against the wall from where he would watch what was going on. He would gradually edge towards the activities once he had been in the room for some time.)
- May become distressed if a familiar routine changes. (Nursery staff were unable to understand why Lucy was so upset until they remembered that they had moved some of the furniture – her favourite comfy chair was no longer in front of the mirror.)
- May impose routines on others. (Leo was never able to leave the house until he'd gone round the living room and touched the arms of each chair.)
- Often engages in stereotypical body movements. (Serena would twirl round and round without even seeming to get dizzy.)
- Often resists new experiences, e.g. trying different foods (Chris would only eat white food like mashed potato and ice cream), wearing new clothes (Gary insisted on wearing the same dungarees every day and his Mum had to buy several identical pairs).
- Finds it hard to work out what other people are going to do, and certainly cannot make sense of why they do things – he is unable to take someone else's perspective.
- Will only develop symbolic play slowly – if at all. (At age four, Robin seemed to have developed a sequence of imaginative play with miniature toys. On further observation it became clear that he just kept repeating the same sequence over and over again. His play lacked imagination.)
- Often pays particular attention to unusual details. (Olivia, in a Reception class, seemed to be engrossed in a group 'Big Book' activity during literacy hour. In fact, her focus was not the story but the telegraph poles she could see in the illustrations.)

In addition, the young child with autism often makes unusual sensory responses of which the following are examples:

- In Nursery, Emma always made a 'beeline' for the water tray where she repeatedly poured water down her forehead – squinting to watch the drips fall from her fringe.
- Natalie, at the Child Development Centre, sniffed and licked each toy before she would pick it up.
- Ricky was hypersensitive to sounds. He couldn't tolerate being in the same room as a vacuum cleaner. He even cried if the next-door neighbours were vacuuming.

Young children with autism have elements of these key features in common, but each child's profile is individual – the Triad of Impairments presenting in different ways in different children. Lorna Wing, cited by Frith (1989), identifies three categories within autism. She describes some children as 'aloof', some as 'passive' and others as 'active but odd'. In addition to these three categories, an important factor influencing the ways in which autism presents is cognitive ability.

The following case studies aim to illustrate the variety of ways in which autism presents in young children.

Case Studies

1. Lucy

Lucy, aged three and a half years, in a private nursery could be described as aloof. She also has significant learning difficulties. It is observed that:

- She generally shuns most physical contact.
- She does not readily cooperate with group activities and displays little social awareness even in familiar situations.
- She shows little attachment to family members, and rarely seeks comfort from them.
- She seems to be unaware of her peers and usually ignores them.
- She has an empty, 'far away' facial expression and avoids direct eye contact.
- She babbles in a monotone voice and sometimes vocalises in a tuneful way, as if singing to herself.
- She is not able to use her vocalisation as a means of communication.
- She will turn towards the source of sounds, but doesn't discriminate between voice and other sounds.
- She engages in repetitive but seemingly aimless activities, e.g. dancing round in circles.
- She shows some obsessional behaviours relating to the watching of particular videos at certain times of day.
- She engages in hand flapping and body twirling.
- She was oblivious to a bicycle wheel going over her foot. Her father reports many incidents of insensitivity to pain.

2. Sebastian

Sebastian is four years old and attends a mainstream nursery school. Although he is aloof, there is evidence that his cognitive abilities fall within the average range. Observations are that:

- He accepts other children around him, but does not initiate contact.
- After 18 months intensive input from a support assistant he begins to initiate some contact with her – especially in 1:1 activities, where he is responding positively to interactive sessions using musical tapes. His Mum has noticed increased eye contact as she plays with him at home.
- His early development of language followed the normal course. He began to babble around 6 months and by 18 months had a vocabulary of 18–20 words. He had stopped talking by the age of two-years.
- He uses a variety of sounds as he undertakes activities. He uses around nine words, but the words are used spasmodically, and are difficult to elicit 'on cue'.
- He has been very preoccupied with letters and numbers and appears to have learned letter names by watching Sesame Street. He sometimes counts 1, 2, 3 . . . as he bounces a ball. He joins in with the 'Thunderbirds' countdown 5, 4, 3, 2, 1, and then says 'go'.
- He is very sensitive to slight changes in routine and to certain sounds. He reacts badly to the unexpected.
- It is very difficult to shift his attention to activities not of his own choosing.
- He doesn't engage in spontaneous imaginative play, but following sessions of structured play he has begun to show elements of basic imaginative play.
- His parents feel he is over-sensitive to sounds.

3. Emily

Aged just 22 months, Emily has weekly visits from the Portage Service. Extremely aloof, her level of cognitive ability has yet to be assessed.

- She dislikes her Mum attempting to play with her.
- Mum is getting quite disheartened as she gets so little feedback from Emily.
- Her favourite activity is listening to music tapes alone in her bedroom.
- When her tape has finished, she stands beside her cassette player and screams until Mum comes to turn the tape over.
- She has tantrums when visitors come to the house – even though they are familiar members of the family.
- Shopping trips are very difficult. Mum tries to go when the shops are quiet as Emily screams if they are crowded.

- The Portage home visitor finds it very hard to get Emily interested in any of the activities she brings. Getting joint attention is almost impossible.
- Mum doesn't know what to get Emily for her birthday as she just doesn't seem interested in toys.

4. Marcus

Marcus, aged four, attends a mainstream nursery. He could be described as passive, but has cognitive abilities within the average range. In detail:

- He doesn't object to other children being around him, but chooses not to join structured group activities. He seems at his most responsive when supported by familiar adults.
- He makes unusual responses to unfamiliar people, e.g. after half an hour with a new teacher, he turned towards her, put his hands on her face, looked into her eyes, smiled, then laughed.
- He prefers not to be approached directly and will respond if given space and time to make the approach himself.
- He begins to use facial expressions to indicate his feelings, e.g. frowning, pouting his lip. These expressions tend to be exaggerated, perhaps because the Support Assistant exaggerated her own facial expressions in order to get them to register with him.
- He will come to Mum for comfort when he's hurt himself, and guide her hand to the spot where it hurts, so that she can rub it better.
- While in range of his Mum, he shows little sign of anxiety. If Mum is not in sight, he becomes very anxious.
- He is beginning to use a combination of eye regard, gesture and vocalisation in order to communicate, e.g., saying 'ye-ye' and nodding his head to either indicate 'yes' or to get an adult to go with him to get something.
- His favourite activity used to be watching videos, but now he just watches for an hour a day. He has started to point out words on the screen.
- He gives full attention and concentrates on tasks which appeal to him. When concentrating, he doesn't respond to sudden loud noises.

5. Malcolm

Malcolm has severe learning difficulties and within Wing's categories could be described as 'active but odd'. Aged almost four, he is in a mainstream nursery.

- His attention is gained by objects rather than social approaches.
- His Mum reports that he has only recently shown awareness of her return after she's been out. He will not interact with other family members.
- He begins to recognise some familiar action games. When his mother says, 'again?' he puts his head on the chair ready to play.
- He has not acquired meaningful speech. He uses the phrase 'bit-a-barbie', saying it quickly when cross, slowly when not. He produces a clicking sound when pleased.
- He does not use gesture to communicate. He will pull people towards objects he wants.
- His Mum reports that he started to scream from birth and spent long periods screaming. He has only recently started to use different sounds for different purposes.
- He has a narrow range of favoured activities, e.g. putting two pegs together, making certain patterns with bricks. Once involved in these activities, he is aware of little else.
- Mum reports that resistance to change is usually what affects his sleep pattern. This can be anything from a change of wallpaper to a change of footwear. She says, 'On certain days I anticipate problems – with new shoes for example – after previously experiencing this three times – only to find that this time he doesn't react! I think I've won the battle of the shoes – only to find that he's deeply upset by the next new pair.'
- He is quite egocentric, pursuing self-directed aims and repetitive activities.

6. Ethan

Although Ethan attends a school for children with moderate learning difficulties, his cognitive abilities are probably within the average range. He could be described as 'active but odd'. He is five years old. Observations are:

- He does not relate to other children in an interactive way and taking turns is very difficult for him. Most of the time he is happy to allow other children alongside him; however, there is one child that he is very aggressive towards.
- He sees adults as tools for his needs. He conforms to their requests in the main. He appears very happy to sit next to an adult and interact in a simple conversation.
- He has made marked progress in the use of language in the months since starting school. However, there is a great deal of repetition of the language of others, repetition of stereotyped phrases and his language is difficult to understand.
- He babbles excitedly at other children; this appears to be to share his delight in electric lights.
- If a child is playing alongside him, he is silently absorbed in what s/he is doing – not in communicating. However, if another child takes one of his toys he squeals loudly.
- He has certain routines that he follows throughout the day, e.g. he has a certain way of getting his drink, and likes to pick up his own pencils and crayons. Interruption of these routines leads to tantrums.
- He displays some obsessive/ritualistic behaviour in school, e.g. he will only go through certain doors, and he will count all the plant pots at the school entrance before he will enter.
- He has to follow certain routines, e.g. if he drops something, he has to pick it up himself or else a tantrum is provoked. Frustration at difficulties with a jigsaw puzzle can rapidly lead to screaming.

Diagnosis

> Diagnosis: 'a signpost, not a label'   (Richard Exley, quoted by Jordan 1999)

Why diagnose?

For some parents and professionals, this may seem a curious question to pose. However, with the advent of the concept of 'Special Educational Needs' (Warnock 1978) and the move away from 'labelling' children, the importance of diagnosis in educational provision has been minimised. Booth (1991), cited by Jordan (1999) for example, claimed that the use of diagnosis in education was discriminatory and overemphasised the child as the source of the difficulties, rather than the educational context. Further concerns included the possible stigmatisation of the child, and a perceived tendency for parents and professionals to accept problems as inevitable and therefore do nothing about them or even to anticipate the occurrence of difficulties and thus potentially contribute to their occurrence and maintenance.

However, for parents, diagnosis can end years of bewilderment, self-blame, distress and frustration. Howlin and Moore (1997) surveyed almost 1,300 parent members of autistic societies in the UK. They found that although children are now being diagnosed earlier than in previous decades, the average age of diagnosis was still around six years, with wide regional variations. However, parents had first become aware that there were developmental problems when the child was around 18 months old, and they began to seek help some six or seven months later. Generally, people first sought help from their GP or Health Visitor, but very few (7.8 per cent) received a diagnosis at this stage. The majority were referred on to other professionals, where a substantial proportion (40 per cent) received a diagnosis. But for more than a quarter there was further delay as they were referred on to yet another professional. For most families there was a delay of more than four years between their first concerns about their child's development and the subsequent diagnosis. The diagnosis came more than three years after they had first sought professional help. One encouraging finding, however, was that children currently under ten years old had been diagnosed (on average) shortly after their fourth birthday. This finding confirms that of Frith and colleagues (1993), who found that 46 per cent of children in their survey of 173 parents were diagnosed between their third and fifth year.

The early provision of a diagnosis ought to lead to early intervention. In their parental survey, Howlin and Moore (1997) found that the amount of support offered following diagnosis was limited. Despite this, 50 per cent of parents were reported to be 'quite satisfied' or 'very satisfied'.

Further, the provision of an accurate diagnosis should allow for a proper orientation of educational strategies. Jordan and Powell (1995) put forward a powerful argument that inclusion can only be effected when individual differences in thinking and learning style are identified and acknowledged in appropriate teaching approaches. In the case of autism, where such differences are pronounced, it is particularly important that they are recognised and taken into account. For professionals, confusion and uncertainty over the best methods of intervention can then be avoided. Although a diagnosis of autism alone would not predetermine educational placement, it is of relevance in determining educational provision. Through acknowledgement in processes such as the statutory assessment leading to a Statement of Special Educational Need, diagnosis can ensure protection of the child's needs. Additionally, diagnosis allows for a degree of prediction as to the possible course of events, though care must be taken to allow for successful intervention in the form of education and therapy. Autism is a lifelong condition and early identification and intervention will enhance opportunities for building on strengths, avoiding secondary behaviour effects and offering strategies for coping – ultimately protecting the individual's lifelong needs.

Difficulties of diagnosis

Most professionals will acknowledge that early identification and diagnosis of autistic spectrum disorders is highly desirable for the reasons outlined above. Why then the delays encountered by parents? Is it timidity on the part of the professional as suggested by one parent in Howlin and Moore's (1997) study, 'I was fed up with professionals pussy-footing around, afraid to say the dreaded word "autism". It seems that the very word "autistic" is taboo.'

Certainly, this may be a factor, since few professionals have the opportunity to see either the full range of autistic spectrum disorders or, indeed, sufficient numbers of children to lead to confidence in recognising and diagnosing the condition. It has been estimated, for example, that GPs will only see one new case of a child with autism during the course of a career.

Autism presents across a series of fine gradations within the spectrum, resulting from the interplay of various factors. Some professionals will have seen neither the numbers nor the range of presentations within the spectrum required to develop the necessary clinical expertise.

Since no blood test, brain scan or identifiable genetic marker yet exists which can make a diagnosis of autism clear-cut, autism can only be recognised by informed observation of behaviour. However, autism cannot be recognised by a single specific behaviour; rather, it is inferred from the interpretation of a pattern of behaviours. Interpretation of behaviour can, of course, be subjective and thus a 'sound background of clinical knowledge' (Frith 1989) is crucial.

Diagnosis of autism thus requires:

- extensive knowledge of normal child development;
- knowledge of abnormal development characterising other conditions, therefore allowing for differentiation;
- the ability to judge the *quality* of impairment;
- systematic checking out of *hypotheses*, that is: *assessment*.

Diagnoses within the autistic spectrum

In 1988 Wing coined the term 'autistic continuum' to convey the notion of a broader clinical phenotype of autism. Diagnostic systems (see below) grouped these under the umbrella term 'Pervasive Developmental Disorders'. During the past ten years there has been growing consensus among clinicians that the range of these disorders does constitute an 'autistic spectrum' (Wing 1997). Thus the synonymous terms Autistic Spectrum Disorders and Pervasive Developmental Disorders refer to a wide range of associated cognitive and neurobehavioural disorders. These are characterised by three defining core features: impairments in socialisation, impairments in verbal and non-verbal communication, together with restricted and repetitive patterns of behaviour.

Pervasive Developmental (Autistic Spectrum) Disorders **DSM IV Diagnoses** (American Psychiatric Association 1994)
Autistic Disorder (Childhood Autism)
Asperger Disorder (Syndrome)
Childhood Disintegrative Disorder
Rett Disorder (Syndrome)
PDD-NOS*/Atypical Autism
(*Pervasive Developmental Disorder – Not Otherwise Specified)

Asperger syndrome

The core difficulties in autism and Asperger syndrome are shared. Asperger syndrome involves a more subtle presentation of difficulties. The key factor given in both DSM IV and ICD 10 to distinguish between autism and Asperger syndrome is the absence of delayed early language development in the latter. However, Wing (1996) notes that some very young children present with what appears to be typical autism, but go on to develop language and other skills, and by adolescence have all the features described by Asperger.

The term Asperger syndrome has been found useful in explaining to parents and teachers the root of the many problems they encounter with a child who, although relatively intellectually able, experiences significant social difficulties (Cumine *et al.* 1998).

Childhood Disintegrative Disorder (CDD)

In this rare condition there is a period of normal development until at least 24 months of age, followed by rapid neurodevelopmental regression resulting in symptoms of autism. Usually CDD occurs between 36 and 48 months. The major signs include loss of previously acquired normal language, social, play, cognitive and motor skills. Alongside this is the onset of stereotypical, repetitive behaviours. In autism, however, clinical regression, when reported, often occurs as early as 15 months. Up to 50 per cent of parents report (usually retrospectively) difficulties within the first year of life. The analysis of family videotapes (e.g. Osterling and Dawson 1994) is helping to clarify issues of 'age of onset'. Nevertheless, difficulties in distinguishing 'age of onset' from 'age of recognition' confuse the picture and the relationship between autism and CDD is poorly understood (Filipek *et al*. 1999)

Rett syndrome

Rett syndrome is a development disorder affecting girls. It is classified under Pervasive Developmental Disorders (PDD) so that a misdiagnosis of autism will not be given. After a period of early normal development during the first 12 months of life there is then a period of rapid deterioration. Particularly noticeable is the loss of purposeful hand movement skills, to be replaced by stereotypical hand movements such as wringing or clapping. Poor truncal or gait coordination appear and there is a loss of social engagement. Cognitive skills and both receptive and expressive language skills are severely impaired.

Atypical Autism/PDD-NOS

Atypical Autism/PDD-NOS is not a distinct clinical entity with a specific definition; rather it is a diagnosis by exclusion of other autistic spectrum disorders. It may be given when the symptoms of autism are only partially present in number or degree, or where the age of onset was over 36 months (American Psychiatric Association 1994). It is worth noting, however, that in one 1996 study quoted by Rapin and others (cited in Filipek *et al*. 1999) of 18 children who had been given a diagnosis of PDD-NOS, there were no significant differences on neuropsychological or behavioural measures from the comparison group who had received a diagnosis of autism.

Differential diagnosis of autistic spectrum disorders

Differential diagnosis of autism includes consideration of:

- generally delayed development and limited cognitive ability;
- specific language disorders;
- psychiatric conditions.

Developmental delay/limited cognitive ability

Young children with severe or profound learning difficulties may present with some of the characteristics of autism, including delayed or absent language, limited eye contact, limited non-verbal communication and possibly stereotyped movements. This overlap of presentation calls for close scrutiny and monitoring of progress and response to intervention during the course of the assessment of very young children.

Specific language disorders

The primary deficits in children with language disorders are in the areas of language and communication. Social skills usually develop despite these. However, in some young children, social interaction and social skill acquisition are severely affected by their language and communication difficulties. Again, there is a need for close scrutiny of the child's social and communicative behaviour and careful monitoring of progress and response to intervention by the multi-professional team.

Some children with complex language and communication difficulties may receive a diagnosis of 'semantic-pragmatic disorder'. Semantic pragmatic disorder was used by Rapin and Allen (1983) to describe a group of language and communication problems in young children, which included receptive language difficulty, echolalia, difficulties with language concepts, inability to use gestures and poverty of symbolic play. However, the much narrower set of diagnostic criteria for autism operating at that time would have ruled out a diagnosis of autism. Given the current breadth of the autistic spectrum, if the complex language disorder involves difficulties in understanding the function of communication as well as semantic and pragmatic difficulties, and if there is also a lack of social empathy and restricted imagination, then the criteria for an autistic spectrum disorder would be met (Jordan 1999). In 1992, Lister-Brooke and Bowler investigated this issue and concluded that semantic-pragmatic disorders do not exist outside the autistic spectrum.

Selective mutism

In this condition, young children may refuse to speak in most situations but will mostly speak in the home context. The history and presentation are usually quite different from autism.

Attachment disorder

This condition occurs following a period of abuse and/or neglect – usually during the first years of life. A child may seem distant and lack social and communication skills, and may have developed stereotyped behaviours, e.g. rocking. However, the difficulties usually respond significantly to appropriate intervention and a more appropriate environment.

Hyperkinetic disorder with stereotypies

In this condition, children have very poor concentration, clumsiness, restlessness and repetitive behaviours, and experience significant learning difficulties. The diagnosis would not be given if the child met the criteria for one of the pervasive developmental disorders.

Landau-Kleffner syndrome

In this condition, children follow a normal developmental course and acquire normal language, but this is followed by a deterioration involving fluctuating loss of speech and is accompanied by epilepsy.

Early diagnosis

It is now possible to diagnose autism before the age of three years. Symptoms of autism are now measurable by the age of 18 months and several research studies have identified the main characteristics which differentiate autism from other developmental disorders occurring in the 20–36 months age range.

Distinguishing impairments are noted in the following areas:

- eye contact;
- orienting to own name;
- joint attention behaviours, e.g. pointing, showing;
- pretend play;
- imitation;
- non-verbal communication;
- language development.

Sensory-perceptual difficulties or repetitive behaviours and behavioural difficulties do not reliably discriminate between children with autism and those experiencing other difficulties (Filipek *et al.* 1999). Nevertheless, early diagnosis presents complex difficulties for the clinician. In one study by Lord (1995) two-year-olds, referred for possible autism, were followed up. It was found that even using a highly reliable diagnostic instrument, the Autism Diagnostic Interview (ADI), discrimination between severe learning difficulties, specific language difficulties and autism was *not* reliable at age two years. In fact the judgement of a (highly experienced) clinician – Lord herself – was more reliable. By age three years, differential diagnosis using the ADI was more reliable. However, the milder or more subtle presentation of Asperger syndrome may still not be reliably distinguished at three years of age. Indeed, some children present at two or three as having autism, but by age seven are regarded as having Asperger syndrome.

Assessment

> The diagnosis of autism as distinct from other developmental disabilities requires a comprehensive multi-disciplinary approach.
> (Filipek *et al.* 1999)

On the basis of systematic analysis of over 2,500 scientific papers by a panel including representatives from nine professional organisations and four parent organisations, the Child Neurology Society and American Academy of Neurology recommended a dual level approach to the diagnosis and evaluation of autism:

1. Routine developmental surveillance.
2. Diagnosis and evaluation.

Detailed recommendations were given for each level. Evaluations should include:

- measures of parental report;
- child observation and interaction;
- clinical judgement.

Assessments should include:

- cognitive;
- adaptive behaviour;
- diagnostic measures.

Multi-disciplinary assessment

The complex and pervasive nature of the difficulties and impairments of autistic spectrum disorders implies the necessity, in establishing good practice in assessment and diagnosis, of involving a range of Early Years professionals. In areas where Child Development Centres exist, the child and family are likely to be seen by a team which may include:

- Consultant Paediatrician/Consultant Community Paediatrician
- Specialist Health Visitor
- Educational and/or Clinical Child Psychologist
- Speech and Language Therapist
- Physiotherapist
- Occupational Therapist
- Early Years teacher
- Social worker
- Nursery nurse/officer.

Additionally, referrals may be made to an Audiology clinic for hearing checks and to a Geneticist to examine for concurrent conditions. Other investigations such as EEGs may, on occasion, be suggested.

Assessment should always include:

- a thorough developmental history;
- background medical information;
- information from any therapeutic intervention undertaken;
- educational history and evaluation of progress;
- child observation and interaction;
- clinical judgement.

Assessment should include information and observation from a range of settings:

- home and family based;
- nursery, preschool or school based;
- specialist settings, e.g. Child Development Centre.

Assessment should be comprehensive and include evaluation of the child's functioning in areas of:

- social interaction;
- social communication;
- social imagination, flexible thinking and play;
- cognitive ability;
- developmental skills in areas of attention control, fine and gross motor functioning and independence skills.

Assessment should also be carried out over time, as functioning can vary from day to day as well as from setting to setting and with different people.

A range of rating scales, checklists, questionnaires, tests and other assessment tools are available to support the processes of assessment and diagnosis. Some of the most commonly used are described in the following section.

Establishing diagnosis

As outlined in the previous chapter, the basis for diagnosis currently is Wing's Triad of Impairments. The full diagnostic criteria for autism according to ICD 10 (WHO 1992) and DSM IV (APA 1994) are given in Appendix 1. It is important to note that these are psychiatric diagnostic criteria which are intended for use by qualified and experienced clinicians, and are not meant to be used as a 'checklist' for autism (Jordan 1999).

Diagnostic systems

Checklist for Autism in Toddlers (CHAT): an early screen for autism

Simon Baron-Cohen and colleagues (1992) have developed a screening tool to be used by health visitors with 18 month old children. It checks for early indications of autism by looking for deficits in the areas of social interaction, communication and play. The CHAT consists of nine questions and five areas of structured observation. Key areas of impaired functioning alert the examiner to the risk of autism and indicate the need for further investigation.

As an instrument, the CHAT is a useful screen. Research study follow-up of children identified (by use of the CHAT) as at risk of having autism has revealed very few 'false positives' (children who seem to have autism at 18 months, but do not on completion of full diagnostic assessment) and 'false negatives' (children who are not identified by the screen at 18 months, but who later receive a diagnosis of autism). Nevertheless the possibility of 'false positives' and 'false negatives' exists and a diagnosis of autism should never be given on the basis of this screening device alone.

Childhood Autism Rating Scale (CARS) Schopler et al. (1988)

The CARS is a structured interview and observation checklist used to investigate the possibility of autism in children over 24 months of age. Fifteen different areas of functioning are examined, using a seven point rating scale to indicate the degree to which the child's behaviour differs from an age-appropriate norm. The total of the ratings on all 15 sub-scales is used to give an indication of the presence or absence of autism and to distinguish mild to moderate from severe autism. It is recommended that the CARS is completed on the basis of:

- perusal of available records;
- information and views from parents;
- information and views from professionals involved, e.g. teachers;
- direct observation.

Jordan (1999) notes that the CARS has been found to have good reliability (over different settings and at different times) and validity (distinguishing those who have autism from those who do not).

The Autism Diagnostic Interview – Revised (ADI–R) Le Couteur et al. (1989)

The ADI is a comprehensive structured parent interview used to build up a picture of how the child functions in areas of communication and language, social development, play and behaviour. Questioning is extremely detailed and non-prejudicial in order to avoid the limitations of earlier checklists which increased the likelihood of positive responses on target behaviours simply by asking only about those behaviours. Scoring procedures provide definitive threshold scores for the diagnosis of autism on the basis of ICD 10 and DSM IV criteria. The ADI is currently the accepted 'gold standard' diagnostic research instrument. Administration of the interview is intended to take one to one and a half hours. However, in practice, administration can take considerably longer than this. Specific training and certification are required in order to administer the ADI.

The Autism Diagnostic Observation Schedule (ADOS) Lord et al. (1989)

The ADOS is a semi-structured observational assessment. Activities are set up to investigate communication, play skills, social interaction, stereotypic behaviour and restricted interests. There are definitive threshold scores which establish a diagnosis of autism against DSM IV and ICD 10 criteria. This schedule is only for those children with a mental age over three years, but a version for younger or less able children has been developed. This is the Pre-linguistic Autism Diagnostic Observation Schedule, PL–ADOS (Di Lavore *et al.* 1995). PL–ADOS allows for freer play and attempts are made to elicit behaviours such as imitation, joint attention and social routines. Specific training is required in the administration of ADOS and PL–ADOS.

Cognitive assessment

Evaluation of the child's level of cognitive functioning is helpful in determining the overall level of functioning and may highlight discrepancies between intellectual ability and social functioning. Assessment of cognitive ability is important in educational planning. However, assessment of young children with autism who may be non-verbal and uncooperative is not straightforward and findings from norm-based tests should be interpreted cautiously. Such tests include the following:

Bayley Scales of Infant Development II (1993)

These scales were devised, as the title suggests, for use with infants up to the age of 42 months, for which norms are given. The scales sample both verbal and non-verbal intellectual skills, and provide an overall index of ability. Norms are current and relatively independent of social function (Filipek *et al.* 1999). The range of play materials used in this assessment includes materials which are attractive to children with autism. Assessment using Bayley Scales is often requested for young children following a Lovaas programme (see Chapter 4).

Leiter International Performance Scales – Revised, Roid and Miller (1997)

The Leiter performance scale was devised as a 'culture-free' non-verbal test and can be used with children from 2–18 years of age. There are four tests at each age level and results yield a mental age or Intelligence Quotient. Its advantages for use with children with autism and communication disorders include the fact that the test is entirely non-verbal, with no verbal instructions given or responses required. Young children find the materials attractive. Some children with autism particularly enjoy the orderliness of inserting the wooden blocks into the wooden stalls, following the same routine for every task. Individual tasks are short, and the test may be administered in 20–30 minutes, but the tasks sample a range of cognitive skills and are graded for difficulty. The test was originally published in 1927 with a revision in 1997 and some of the pictorial material now appears very dated. Test scores of younger children and those with moderate to severe learning difficulties are sometimes over-optimistic in terms of predicting future functioning.

Psycho-educational Profile – Revised (PEP–R), Schopler et al. (1990)

The PEP–R offers a developmental approach to the assessment of children with autism or related developmental disorders from six months of age. The PEP–R links closely with the TEACCH (Treatment and Education of Autistic and Communication handicapped CHildren) intervention approach, which will be discussed more fully in Chapter 4.

The child's development in a number of areas is examined using a range of materials which are particularly appealing to children with autism. There are sub-scale scores in the areas of imitation, perception, motor skills, eye–hand coordination, cognitive and verbal skills. Further sub-scales, assessed by observation of the child during the assessment, include atypical behaviours and sensory functioning.

Performance on PEP–R is intended to inform the design of individual education plans for children within the TEACCH approach (Schopler 1984). Ratings thus include the category of 'emerging' skill as well as 'pass' or 'fail'. Overall Developmental Quotients can be calculated, but this is a ratio measure based on a small sample size.

Social and adaptive behaviour

The main tool currently used to assess adaptive behaviour is the Vineland Adaptive Behaviour Scales.

The Vineland Adaptive Behaviour Scales, Sparrow et al. (1984)

These scales , widely used in the USA, are being used increasingly in the UK in the assessment of adaptive behaviour as they are always a required part of assessment for children following a Lovaas programme (see pp. 39, 48/9 below). Three versions are available: a survey form, an expanded interview form and a classroom form. The expanded interview is most useful for children with autism and supplementary norms have recently been published for children with autism (Carter *et al.* 1998). Standard scores, percentile ranks, adaptive levels and age equivalents are available. The scales investigate the presence of developmentally ordered skills in four domains:

- socialisation (interpersonal relationships, play and leisure time, coping skills);
- daily living skills (personal, domestic and community skills);
- motor skills (gross and fine motor);
- communication (receptive, expressive and written).

The detailed interview is carried out with parents.

Communication and language skills

As with other areas, assessment of the communication and language skills of children with autism is difficult because most assessment scales assume a typical or 'normal' developmental path, whereas in autism, the pattern of development is deviant rather than delayed. Formal assessment procedures must be complemented by structured observational approaches. In the early years, the following published checklists may be helpful in building up a picture of a child's communication skills:

The Pre-verbal Communication Schedule, Kiernan and Reid (1987)

This schedule is particularly useful for young or less able children with autism, concentrating on pre-verbal forms of communication. Negative forms of communication, such as temper tantrums, are included as well as positive indications of attempts to communicate. Pre-intentional forms of communication are also examined, allowing for the identification of behaviour which could be shaped into intentional communication.

The Pragmatic Profile of Early Communication Skills, Dewart and Summers (1988)

Information on the young child's use of language and communication is gained by interviewing parents and others significantly involved with the child. Communicative functions assessed include:

- responses made to the communicative approaches of others, e.g. understanding gestures, understanding a speaker's intentions;

- reactions in conversational situations, e.g. initiation and maintenance of conversation;
- how he communicates in different contexts.

The range of skills covered is comprehensive in terms of communicative functions, so that the completed profile highlights areas which may be targets for intervention.

Speech and Language Therapists may additionally use standardised assessments including:

- British Picture Vocabulary Scales, which are used to assess receptive vocabulary.
- Clinical Evaluation of Language Functioning, which is used to assess receptive and expressive language ability, e.g. sentence structure, basic concepts, formulating labels, recalling sentences.
- Test of Reception of Grammar (TROG), which is used to assess comprehension of more advanced language structures.
- The Derbyshire Language Scheme, which provides a qualitative approach to assessment and forms a basis for intervention.

Play-based assessment

Elizabeth Newson, as Director at Nottingham University's Child Development Research Unit, pioneered the use of play-based assessment. In 1979 she wrote:

> In a sense, when we assess a child on formal tests we confine him within the tramlines of our own preconceptions about the nature of the abilities that he might show . . . For children with uneven and anomalous development, and for those with serious problems in behaviour and in social relationships, it is likely to be dangerous and misleading, because these children have already shown us that our tramlines are just what they cannot run on.

Newson therefore advises 'detailed and sensitive observation of a child's spontaneous or responsive play' as a more potent source of information about the child. 'Naturalistic but well-managed play sessions can enable a child to demonstrate not only his ability to solve formal problems, but his approach to and strategies in, the kind of problem solving that naturally arises in play.'

Newson goes on to suggest a variety of toys, materials and activities which may elicit a child's responses in the following areas:

- imitation;
- following instructions;
- reciprocal (turn-taking) play;
- manipulative skills;
- gross motor function;
- speech and communication;
- cognitive skills;
- symbolic (pretend) play.

For the independent professional examiner who is new to the child, Newson suggests the judicious use of toys such as bubbles, a marble run, balloons, pop-up cones, musical box or a humming top to attract the child into the play situation.

The involvement of parents is advised. In assessments conducted by Professor Newson, parents are able to observe their child's performance through a two-way mirror. Through discussions with parents and, if possible, enlisting the involvement of parents, a fuller picture will be gained of the child's abilities, skills and areas of difficulty.

Early Years practitioners are ideally placed to carry out play-based observations in semi-structured situations over time – if they are clear about what they are looking for! The following set of suggestions are intended to help the Early Years practitioner in gathering information regarding the child's functioning, skill levels and aspects of behaviour relevant in the assessment of autistic spectrum disorders in young children.

Contribution of parents and Early Years practitioners to assessment and diagnosis in autism

Parents, together with Early Years teachers and other nursery and playgroup staff, can help in providing information for professionals involved in diagnosing and assessing autistic spectrum disorders. Early Years practitioners will make their usual observations and assessment in playgroup, nursery or infant class, but in addition it will be helpful to make specific observations in three key areas of development.

1. Social interaction

Does the child:

- Look at you when you are talking to him or doing things together?
- Follow your gaze when you look at something?
- Allow you to amuse him without using toys?
- Raise his arms in anticipation of being lifted up?
- Smile back at you if you smile at him?
- Smile in greeting when being collected from nursery/playgroup?
- Wave 'bye bye' – in imitation? – spontaneously?
- Offer or show you things that interest him?
- Sometimes tease you, e.g. 'offer' you something and then take it back?
- Point with his finger to indicate interest in something (as opposed to indicating desire to have the item)?
- Look back at you when he's pointing?
- Look at you and/or vocalise to get your attention?
- Become excited and happy and try to share this feeling with you?
- Come for a cuddle when asked? – or only on his terms?
- Share toys, activities, sweets with you and with other children?
- Seem to share in your pleasure or excitement?
- Ever try to comfort someone who is upset?
- Come for comfort when hurt or upset?
- If upset, calm down when spoken to softly? If not – how can he be calmed?
- Show emotions on his face, e.g. by frowning, looking guilty or surprised?
- Understand emotions shown on the faces of others?
- Give hugs and kisses spontaneously to close family members?
- Show shyness or anxiety when meeting unfamiliar people?
- Look towards other children or adults who approach him showing pleasure, or does he turn away showing anxiety or distress?
- Ever 'check back' to see if his carer is still there/still watching him?
- Take turns in games, e.g. ball games?
- Imitate simple actions or sequences of actions?

2. Social communication

Does the child:

- Have a way of letting you know he wants something – using sounds, words or gestures, or by leading you by the hand or wrist?
- Respond when his name is called?
- Look at you, then at the object he wants and then look back at you, while trying to let you know what he wants?
- Point to indicate something he wants, looking back as he points?
- Follow your points to items nearby, or in the distance?
- Nod his head to indicate 'yes' or shake it for 'no'?
- Use sounds or words or strings of sounds as if to join in a conversation when you talk to him?
- Use clear words? What are they? Has he ever lost words from his vocabulary?
- Tell you if he's hurt himself, and let you know how it happened?
- Repeat certain phrases he's heard or made up, e.g. 'bit-a-barbie'?
- Repeat learned strings of words, or chunks of speech from TV or videos?
- Ever say the same thing over and over again, or try to get you to say the same thing again and again.
- Ask questions to build on what you or others have said, or simply stick to his own topic?
- Ever get pronouns mixed up, e.g. saying 'Do you want a biscuit?', but meaning, 'I want a biscuit'?
- Ever show an interest in the whereabouts or doings of others in the family or nursery / playgroup?
- Bring items on request from another room?

3. Play and flexible behaviour

Does the child:

- Show interest in new toys or books? How does he react?
- Have any particular favourite toys, books, videos?
- Play appropriately with toys, e.g. pushing a car along the floor, going 'brrm brrm'; build a tower of bricks, or fill a bucket with sand?
- Tend to sniff or mouth objects, or squint at things?
- Play any pretend games with dolls, cars, trains, action figures, or in the 'home corner'?
- Play 'pretend' – but it's the same play sequence repeated again and again?
- Ever play at 'pretend' with other children?
- Enjoy (or has enjoyed when younger) playing 'peek a boo' or hide and seek?
- Show any interest in other children – either coming to the house, or at nursery / playgroup?
- Join in any games with other children, e.g. hide and seek, or ball games?
- Have any particularly unusual special interests, e.g. in asking about microwave ovens, noticing telegraph poles?
- Become interested in certain parts of a toy, e.g. turning a car upside down to spin its wheels?
- Ever line up items in play, e.g. cars, farm animals?
- Get upset if there are minor changes to his routine, e.g. going to playgroup by a different route?
- Establish his own routines, e.g. insisting on going to MacDonald's every time he's out in the car?
- Insist on following certain rituals, e.g. touching furniture in a particular order before leaving the house?
- React with distress to relatively ordinary sounds, e.g. coughing?

21

- Moves his hands or fingers in an odd or unusual way – flapping/flicking?
- Walk on tip-toes, or have any unusual body mannerisms?

Early Years assessment scenarios

Some scenarios typical of Early Years settings are outlined on the following pages. These can provide very natural assessment opportunities when observing/interacting with a child thought to have an autistic spectrum disorder. Together with a description of each scenario, there is guidance on:

- what to look out for;
- how to extend the observation through intervention.

Summary

- There is no simple test or checklist which will confirm the diagnosis of autism.
- The presence of autism is inferred on the basis of interpretation of a pattern of behaviours.
- The boundaries of autism overlap other conditions and an awareness of the issues of differential diagnosis is essential.
- Adequate assessment and diagnosis of autism will involve a range of professionals from various disciplines.
- Early Years practitioners and parents can provide vital information to assist the assessment process.
- Specialised tools exist which may inform the assessment, but the role of qualitative, play-based assessment is crucial.

1. Sand/water tray

What to look out for:

Does the child tolerate other children standing beside him? Does he tolerate just one or two, but leave if more join in?

Does he watch what the other children do and try to copy them?

How does he respond if they try to talk to him?

Does he strongly object to wearing an apron?

Does he negotiate for the buckets etc. he wants, or just grab them?

Does he repeat the same action over and over, e.g. tipping sand into a bucket that's already full?

Does he do anything unusual, e.g. holding his arm up, sprinkling sand in front of his eyes, watching as it falls?

How to extend:

Call his name as he is engrossed in the sand/water play – does he respond?

Play beside him. Imitate what he is doing. Does he notice?

Gently intervene in his play. If he's sprinkling sand, or pouring water – catch it in a container. Does he 'let you in'?

Get each of the other children to imitate a simple action, e.g. pouring water into a funnel – can you get the target child to take his turn and imitate you too?

Have a sand/water free day – how does the child react if his favourite activity is unavailable?

Have the sand tray out, but none of the usual buckets and spades – let it be a dinosaur landscape instead – with miniature dinosaurs. Can he go along with the change? Can he enter into the pretend play with the model dinosaurs?

2. Outdoor play
What to look out for:
Does the child prefer to stay on the edge of the play area, or does he use all the space available?
Does he like to walk round and round following a specific route? What happens if someone is blocking his way?
Does he find things on the ground (e.g. an insect or a leaf) and bring them to show you?
Does he ever approach any of the other children? What happens if they go up to him?
How to extend:
Roll a ball gently towards his feet; does he roll or kick it back?
Point to a plane or a bird in the sky; does he look towards it?
Prompt other children to play a simple game, e.g. 'tig'. Does he join in?

3. Home corner
What to look out for:
Does he ever go to this area, or does he avoid it?
Is he able to use the scaled-down equipment appropriately, e.g. putting a pan on the 'cooker'? Or does he just treat the 'cooker' as a cupboard, piling toys into it?
Does he engage in role-play with others?
Does he ever think the pretend 'food' is real and try to eat it?
Does he have a particular fascination for the mirror?
How to extend:
Play alongside him. Pretend to cook/lay the table/wash up. Does he watch you? Can he be encouraged to take a turn?
Have some dressing up hats available near the mirror. Will he try one on and look at himself? Will he show you what he looks like? Will he pull faces in the mirror?

4. Toy cars/train set
What to look out for:
Is this a favourite activity?   Can he tolerate anyone sharing the activity?   Does he always insist on the same layout?   Does he line the cars and trains up, or can he be more imaginative?
How to extend:
Play alongside him. If he's lining things up, put one of your cars/trains in his line. How does he react?   Make car/train noises – does he imitate you?   Place a car at the top of a ramp. Say 'Ready, Steady . . . Go' before releasing the car. Repeat the sequence. Just say, 'Ready, Steady . . .' and pause. Will he say 'Go'?

3 Implications of current theories for intervention

Organic explanations for autism

Evidence for an organic cause for autism

There has been a growing body of evidence, described as 'overwhelming' by Francesca Happe (1994), to suggest that autism has an organic cause. Although Kanner (1943) had hinted at a biological link in autism it was Rutter's (1978) study which emphasised the involvement of organic brain dysfunction. Rutter found that one quarter of his sample of children with autism developed epilepsy in adolescence and one third had raised serotonin levels. Olsson *et al.* (1988) also found a high incidence of epilepsy in a sample of children with autism, and Steffenburg and Gillberg (1990) found that around 90 per cent of their sample of 35 children with autism and 17 children with an 'autistic-like' condition showed evidence of brain damage or dysfunction.

Further evidence for an organic cause is the association between general learning difficulties and autism. Excluding children with Asperger syndrome, three quarters of children with autism also have learning difficulties; that is, on general intelligence testing they are found to have an IQ below 70 (Rutter 1979). The implication is that if autism results from damage to a specific area or areas of the brain, then widespread damage leading to general learning difficulties would be likely also to affect those areas causing autism. Indeed, research indicates that the more severe the learning difficulty, the more likely is the association with autism (Smalley *et al.* 1988). Other features indicating the likely organic basis to autism are that it is found with a similar frequency in different cultures.

Although it is *not* the case that all children with autism will experience epilepsy or severe learning difficulties, and in the majority of children there are no associated medical conditions, when *groups* of children are studied, various medical conditions feature more often than would be expected.

The implication then is that some biological cause is likely to account for autism, although this is rarely identifiable (Baron-Cohen and Bolton 1993). Although no precise site of a lesion or disrupted neurochemical pathway can be identified, it is now confidently asserted that autism has a primary cause at the level of the brain (Steffenburg and Gillberg 1990). Gillberg and Coleman (1992) describe autism and related disorders as biologically determined behavioural syndromes with varying aetiology.

Genetic causes of autism

The idea of a genetic component to autism has been substantiated by recent research. Population studies (Lotter 1966, Wing and Gould 1979, Ehlers and Gillberg 1993) have indicated that autism is much more common in boys than girls and autism is 50 times more frequent in the brothers and sisters of people with autism than in the general population (Folstein and Rutter 1979; Smalley *et al.* 1988). The proof that genetic factors are involved though comes from twin studies. Identical (monozygotic) twins, since they come from the same fertilised egg, are genetically identical, whereas non identical (dizygotic) twins develop from two separately fertilised eggs and are, therefore, similar to any brother or sister pair, in sharing only half of their genes. In twin studies in autism, the rate of both twins having autism in identical twins is significantly higher than the rate in non-identical twins. This provides evidence for genetic causality in autism. However, even in identical twins if one twin has autism, the other does not necessarily have it (Folstein and Rutter 1977; Le Couteur *et al.* 1996).

Some studies have found more general difficulties in language, reading difficulties and learning difficulties in the twin without autism (Baron-Cohen and Bolton 1993). Others have found social and communication difficulties in the brothers and sisters of people with autism (August *et al.* 1981, Bolton *et al.* 1994, cited in Jordan 1999). This has led to the notion of the 'extended phenotype' in autism.

Genetic conditions that can produce autism

Baron-Cohen and Bolton (1993) list the following rare conditions that can sometimes, but not always, lead to autism:

- Fragile X syndrome
- Phenylketonuria (PKU)
- Tuberous sclerosis
- Neurofibromatosis
- Cornelia de Lange syndrome
- Noonan syndrome
- Coffin Siris syndrome
- William's syndrome
- Biedl-Bardet syndrome
- Moebius syndrome
- Leber's amaurosis.

Of these conditions, Fragile X features most prominently in its association with autism, in that 26 per cent of the Fragile X population children with severe learning difficulties also have autism. However, fewer than 10 per cent of the population with autism when screened, are found to carry the Fragile X gene (Trevarthen *et al.* 1996). This is a relatively small percentage, but it does make Fragile X one of the most common causes of autism identified so far.

Autism sometimes occurring in children born with PKU has become very rare since all children born in the UK are tested for it in the first week of life and treatment started immediately. This treatment prevents the brain damage which would otherwise occur due to the build up of toxins.

A significant connection has been found between tuberous sclerosis and autism. Tuberous sclerosis is a neurological disorder with behavioural manifestations. It is characterised by the growth of benign tumours, unusual skin pigmentation and a particular facial rash. Gillberg *et al.* (1994) estimated that 9 per cent of individuals with autism have tuberous sclerosis, especially where epilepsy and general learning difficulties also exist. Thus the connection may be via the brain damage rather than through a genetic link. Smalley *et al.* (1988) report that studies of tuberous sclerosis indicate autistic features to be present in 17–58 per cent of subjects (also see Gillberg and Coleman 1992).

Neurofibromatosis was first specifically described in association with autism by Gillberg and Forsell (1984). This is a genetic condition affecting the nerves and skin, where learning difficulties can occur in association with brain damage. It can be recognised by the appearance of café au lait (brown) spots on the trunk and limbs of the body. It is not known why children with neurofibromatosis may also develop autism.

More detailed discussion of the syndromes associated with autism can be found in Gillberg and Coleman (1992)

Recent work on the biology of autism

Recent work on the biology of autism has led to the suggestion that food metabolism may be affected and that thus the chemical environment of the brain is affected. These theories propose that there is an inability to metabolise certain foods adequately, leading to harmful toxins entering the brain. According to Shattock (1998) the child is unable to tolerate casein from milk and gluten from wheat (or both) and the endogenous opioid system is affected.

Conclusions

There are many contenders to be the 'cause' of autism, with clear evidence for an organic basis to the condition and substantial indications of the role of genetic factors. There may be several different causes, which all result in the same area or areas of the brain being affected, but the existence of autism as a syndrome does not depend on a single organic cause or a single gene being found. Autism is diagnosed at the level of behaviour. It is characterised at the level of psychological functioning; that is, it is the disordered functioning of the brain which leads to the characteristic behaviours of autism. It is through increasing our understanding at this, psychological, level that we as educators can make a difference. As Francesca Happe writes, 'we are still a long way from pinpointing the area of damage in the autistic **brain**, but it may be that we can specify what function is lost in the autistic **mind**'.

From theories to intervention

> Human beings are born psychologists . . . Far from being something which baffles human understanding, the open discussion of one's inner experience is literally child's play to a human being, something which children begin to learn before they are more than two or three years old.
> (Humphrey 1984, in Baron-Cohen 1995)

Autism as a disorder has baffled and fascinated investigators since it was first identified by Kanner. The peculiar nature of the problem is that it is not visible in the way that a physical difficulty is. And, in contrast to sensory deficits, the sources of the difficulties are not obvious. Autism is inferred purely on the basis of its behavioural effects and the patterns and combinations of these behaviours observed in varying contexts. Despite extensive research into the biological nature of autism and its genetic bases, it is still not possible to pinpoint with certainty the area or areas of damage in the autistic brain, much less the pathway from the brain to the behaviours. However, during the last decade or so some extremely interesting theories have emerged attempting to explain what may be lost, altered, preserved or even enhanced in the developing mind of the young child with autism.

To us as educators theoretical explanations of the difficulties inherent in autism are not merely interesting; they are, indeed, vital to our practice. Without a coherent working model of the processes which may be at work to produce the behaviours typical of autism, we are reduced as educators to a piecemeal approach, tackling individual behaviours one at a time, or following 'recipes' for successful teaching. The problem with the latter approach is that when a difficulty occurs because the child does not respond as suggested by the 'recipe', the teacher has no framework of understanding or underlying principles to help guide amended or alternative strategies. Ironically, as Powell and Jordan (1997) crisply state, 'such educationists then find themselves in the same position as an individual with autism: unable to step outside of the learned routine and at a loss as to how to proceed next.'

Along with Jordan and Powell (1995) the present authors, therefore, would argue for an educational approach that takes full account of the specific 'autistic' way of thinking and learning, and for autism as a different culture – another dimension.

In outlining the following proposed explanations or models of functioning in autism at the psychological level, it is the authors' intention that they should serve for the reader as a set of lenses through which autism may be perceived. In our previous book (Cumine *et al.* 1998) we used the image of the Asperger lens to invite the reader to note how behaviours interpreted from an ordinary, non-autistic, point of view will look very different when viewed from the point of view of the person with autism. More importantly, our responses to the behaviour are dramatically altered. In arriving at an understanding of the world from the viewpoint of the person with autism it is our contention that several 'lenses' of interpretation may need to be tried. Rather as on a visit to the optician, several different lenses will be inserted, sometimes separately, sometimes in combination, in order to bring the letter chart into clear focus.

One thing is absolutely certain: in stark contrast to Humphrey's statement heading this part of the chapter, human beings with autism are absolutely *not* born psychologists.

In his original work, Kanner (1943) suggested that autism resulted from 'an innate inability to form the usual *biologically provided affective contact* with people'. In this way he indicated that emotional relatedness to others is usually a 'given'. Ordinarily the child is born with this ability and does not have to *learn* how to relate socially and emotionally to fellow human beings. However, this insight was lost for a period of time when Bettelheim (1956) claimed that autism consisted of 'a disturbance of the ability to reach out to the world' as a result of a lack of parental emotional warmth, coining the term 'refrigerator parent'. These theories have since been entirely discredited on two main grounds. Firstly, researchers point to normally developing siblings of autistic children – unaffected by so-called 'refrigerator parents'. Secondly, children who have suffered extensive emotional neglect, once 'rescued', do develop the ability to communicate and interact with others (Clarke and Clarke 1976).

Subsequently it has been argued that linguistic difficulties give rise to the social difficulties in autism, together with the behavioural challenges. It is only relatively recently, however, that attention has shifted back to the *social* nature of the difficulties in autism as being at the 'core' of the disorder. Wing and Gould's 1979 study identified the Triad of Impairments in Social Interaction, Social Communication and Social Imagination and Behaviour as crucial in defining the disorder, in that they are universal among all those with autism and not present in other groups.

This focus on the social nature of the core difficulties sets the stage for the development of research into impaired theory of mind functioning in autism.

'Theory of Mind'

In attempting to explain the universal and specific features of autism, more recent theories have focused on the proposed impairment of the fundamental human ability to 'mind-read'. Normally developing children, from around the age of four years, are able to understand (however implicitly) that other people have thoughts, beliefs, intentions and desires which impel their behaviour. They are also able to recognise that individuals vary in their thoughts, beliefs, intentions and desires, and that these differences will lead to differences in behaviours. The 'Theory of Mind' explanation of autism proposes that this ability is specifically impaired in autism, that people with autism do not develop the ability to think about others' thoughts so that they are specifically impaired in certain (but not all) social, communicative and imaginative skills (Happe 1994). However, 'it is not just that children with autism do not understand *what* others are thinking and feeling but that they do not understand *that* they are thinking and feeling' (Jordan 1999).

This account of the difficulties in autism is based on the now widely known 'Sally–Anne' experiment carried out by Baron-Cohen *et al.* in 1985 (see Figure 3.1). This could also be described as a 'false belief' task. False belief is a clear example of a mental state which exists separately from the reality of the situation.

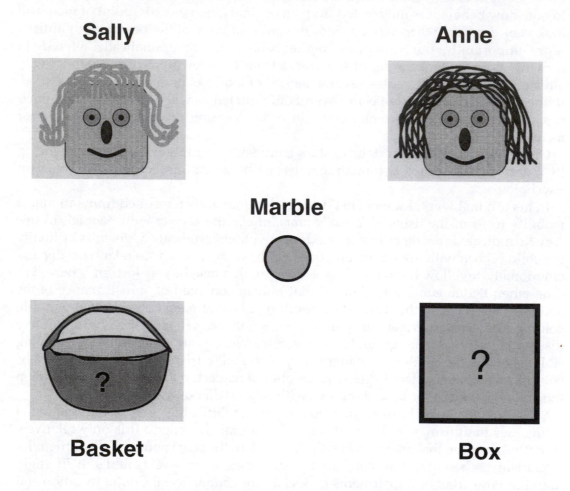

Figure 3.1 Sally, Anne and the marble (Baron-Cohen *et al.* 1985)

Twenty children with autism with mental ages well over four years were compared in their performance on this task with a group of children with Down's syndrome of a slightly lower average mental age, and with a group of normally developing four year olds. The children watch as the experimenter manipulates two dolls, Sally who has her basket, and Anne who has a box, in the performance of a short story. This consists of Sally placing a marble in her basket then leaving the room. While she is out, Anne takes the marble from Sally's basket and places it in her own box. Sally then returns and the child is asked, 'Where will Sally look for her marble?'

Eighty per cent of the children with autism failed to understand that Sally could not know where the marble was, i.e. that her actions would be based on a false belief. These children replied that she would look in the box, where the marble *actually* was, rather than in the basket where she *believed* it to be. In contrast, 86 per cent of the Down's children (12 out of 14) passed the test correctly, stating (as did the normally developing four year olds) that Sally would look in her basket. This result has been replicated many times. The experiment seemed to reveal an impairment which was specific and unique to the condition of autism, an impairment in the ability to understand that people have mental states which can be different from the world of reality and that can be different from one's own. Further, the question arises regarding the ability of those with autism to recognise that they themselves have mental states and how and to what extent this awareness may be developed.

In his book *Mindblindness* (1995), Simon Baron-Cohen details experimental findings of allied difficulties in autism: understanding that seeing leads to knowing; understanding deception; recognising belief-based emotions; understanding the brain as an organ with mental functions; distinguishing appearance and reality. An example of the latter is that if shown a stone which looks like an egg, children with autism will say that it really is an egg.

Baron-Cohen goes on to say that if children with autism are unaware of the appearance/reality distinction and are unaware that they and other people have thoughts about the world, then their world must be dominated by current perceptions and sensations unfiltered, as it were, by a lens of interpretation. The social world (guided, interpreted, created as it is by our thinking about our own and other people's motives, beliefs, desires and intentions) must be a very frightening place for them.

Alison Gopnik (1993), cited by Baron Cohen (1995), imagined what it must be like to look at the world through the eyes of someone who is 'mind-blind':

> This is what it's like to sit round the dinner table. At the top of my field of vision is a blurry edge of nose, in front are waving hands . . . Around me bags of skin are draped over chairs, and stuffed into pieces of cloth. They shift and protrude in unexpected ways . . . Two dark spots near the top of them swivel restlessly back and forth. A hole beneath the spot fills with food and from it comes a stream of noises. Imagine that the noisy skin bags suddenly moved towards you, and their noises grew loud, and you had no idea why, no way of explaining them and predicting what they would do next.

This conveys graphically what the world may seem like to the young child with autism, and evokes an understanding of the state of alarm in which the young child may, and indeed often does, seem to live. Parents of young children with autism often refer to their extreme state of tension and fearfulness.

Implications of 'theory of mind' impairment for the young child with autism

In normally developing children, 'theory of mind' is acquired around the age of four years. However, the difficulties of autism do not 'spring into being' as the young child hits four. They are apparent much earlier than that and usually are causing great anxiety and concern by the time the child is around 18 months old. At this age, the child's behaviour often appears incomprehensibly stubborn, fearful, aggressive, rigid. Communication and language fail to develop and, in contrast to his peers, the child fails to develop early pretend play, clinging instead to rigid repetitive patterns of actions with objects, such as spinning or lining them up.

Baron-Cohen (1995) has gone on to propose the precursors to 'theory of mind' in early development, based on an innate 'mind-reading instinct'. Firstly, he suggests that children with autism **are** able to develop understanding about people wanting things. He also suggests that they are able to detect eye direction, for example in photographs (although, as Jordan (1999) points out, there is a great deal of evidence that gaze monitoring is not spontaneous in children with autism).

Baron-Cohen then goes on to suggest the major area of difficulty to be that of 'shared attention' leading to joint referencing. Joint referencing is the ability to follow the direction of another person's eye regard or the direction of a pointed finger, and to recognise the indicated object as an object of shared attention. Similarly, by looking at an object or pointing to it, the other person's attention can be enlisted. This three way process forms the basis of communication (see Figure 3.2).

The ability to engage in shared attention, Baron-Cohen maintains, is the prerequisite for theory of mind to develop. Since this ability is impaired in autism, and the child is unable to engage in shared attention, theory of mind fails to develop. Approaches to teaching young children with autism, such as musical interaction (see Chapter 4), build upon the need to encourage the development of shared attention.

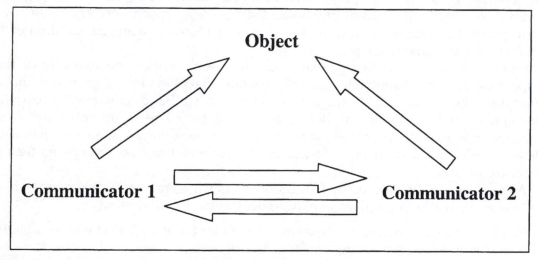

Figure 3.2 Communication – a three way process

Intersubjectivity

Other theorists maintain that the impaired theory of mind explanation of autistic functioning neglects the role of emotion. Kanner (1943) described autism as a 'disturbance of affective contact'. Hobson (1993) maintains that children do not develop a 'theory of mind', but rather, they build up a knowledge of other people as having minds through their intersubjective experience. Human infants, in Hobson's view, are born with a predisposition to relate to emotional expression, an ability to respond naturally with feelings to the feelings, expressions, gestures and actions of others. These biologically given 'pre-wired' capacities for direct perception of others' emotions and attitudes allow us to begin to develop an understanding of others as separate beings with their own feelings, thoughts, beliefs and attitudes. The development of the concepts of 'self' and 'other', able to share and also to differ in feelings, thoughts, beliefs and attitudes, is a necessary prerequisite to the development of 'theory of mind' functioning. For Hobson, 'to understand minds is also to understand the nature of selves who have minds'.

In a similar vein, Meltzoff and Gopnik (1993) argue that early imitation is impaired in autism, particularly imitation of facial expressions. It is through this mutual imitation of emotional expressions that the concepts of 'self' and 'other' are built up – 'the face bone is connected to the mind bone' as they put it. If mutual imitation is impaired, then development of the concepts of 'self' and 'other' will be impaired likewise.

The difficulty children with autism have in understanding emotional expression in themselves and others can be extremely striking. Ross, aged five, when asked to 'give me a smile' put his fingers to the corners of his mouth and lifted them up. Craig, aged six, in the middle of piteous sobbing, paused to squint at the teardrops on his eyelashes. Jake, aged nine, would not acknowledge that he cried – when tears came he tried to push them back in (see Figure 3.3). When Jake's mother asked him to draw a picture of himself in tears, he insisted on drawing a girl crying – so that it didn't look like him.

Figure 3.3 Jake, pushing the tears back in

An 'experiencing self'

Further developing the implications of difficulties in the intersubjective domain, and building on the experience of difficulties in emotional expression, emotional experience and emotional learning, Powell and Jordan (1993) proposed a difficulty in establishing an 'experiencing self' as fundamental to autism. This suggestion arose from the difficulties noted in children with autism in developing a 'personal episodic memory' or a personal memory for events. That is, they have difficulty in experiencing events subjectively and then being able to recall them. Without this 'experiencing self', events would be coded 'from the outside' in a non-subjective way, and this is how the person with autism often does seem to experience events. Jordan (1999) quotes Temple Grandin (1995), an adult person with autism, 'When I access my own memory, I see many different "videos".'

Implications of impaired theory of mind for Early Years practice

- The young child with autism can be helped to *make sense of the social behaviour of others* by building in predictability, through clarity of the physical environment and by using tangible and visual cues and clues.
- The young child with autism will often *lack the motivation to please others*. The usual social reinforcers, such as praise, are unlikely to be effective. It is important to use motivators which appeal to the child with autism, perhaps building in the use of the child's own special interests, e.g. offering a Thomas the Tank Engine toy once a given task has been completed.
- Given that young children with autism *have difficulty in understanding emotion* it would be surprising if they readily responded to emotional warmth in an adult's voice, or to a frown of disapproval. There will be opportunities, however, to exaggerate emotional expressions and to draw the child's attention to it, e.g. 'Jamie's fallen over. He's hurt his knee. He's crying. Look at his sad face.'
- To extend a child's ability to *share attention* and give *meaningful eye contact*, 'Intensive interaction' and 'Music supported interaction' strategies can be useful, together with directly teaching pointing skills – close range pointing first, followed by distant pointing, encouraging 'pointing to share' as well as 'pointing to request'. It is important to begin with the adult sharing the child's attention, before helping the child to share the adult's focus of attention.
- Because the young child with autism *finds it hard to make sense of social rules and conventions*, key sub-skills, e.g. turn-taking, need to be taught before the child can be expected to learn in a group. These can be developed via physical 'to and fro' games with balls, balloons and bubbles, and by using musical games.
- Attempts to develop the child's *sense of an experiencing self* begin at the physical level – perhaps performing actions in front of a mirror. Later, photographs (and video if available) are useful in helping to record the child's experience of common events, developing his awareness of self-involvement in the creation of a memory.

Carol Gray (2000) describes techniques for helping young children recall and relate recent experiences. Parents are asked to send their children into school with a zipped 'freezer' bag containing real items from weekend or evening or holiday activities. A bus ticket and some empty sweet wrappers could help the child explain that he'd been to Grandma's, while a few acorns and dried leaves could help him describe a country walk. Gray finds this technique preferable to the commonly used home–school diary as it provides the child with tangible cues to help him retrieve personal memories.

Weak central coherence

Central coherence is the term coined by Uta Frith (1989) for the tendency we all have to try to extract and remember the 'gist' of a conversation or story, or to form a picture of a 'whole' rather than the individual parts – pulling information together for meaning as opposed to recalling individual elements. This tendency enables us to accurately recognise words with ambiguous meanings through awareness of the context in which they occur. For example 'the sun is shining today' would not be understood as 'the son is shining today'. Frith has suggested that this global processing is disturbed in autism, where detail-focused processing dominates instead. This can be seen in the way that children with autism often play with parts of toys (e.g. the wheels of a car) rather than the whole thing, or in the way that they focus on small irrelevant details (e.g. a speck of fluff on the carpet).

Kanner (1943) commented on this fragmentary processing and its role in the child with autism's resistance to change. 'A situation, a performance, a sentence is not regarded as complete if it is not made up of exactly the same elements that were present at the time the child was first confronted with it.'

The 'weak central coherence' theory of autism attempts to explain and predict skills as well as impairments. Shah and Frith (1993) demonstrated that children with autism were unusually good at the block design sub-test of the Wechsler Intelligence Scale for Children (WISC). In this task, the child is presented with a number of blocks, the surfaces of which are either entirely red, entirely white, or half red/half white. These then have to be assembled to resemble a given pattern as in Figure 3.4. Shah and Frith maintain that the skilfulness of children with autism is specifically related to their segmentation abilities. For the rest of us, the task is difficult because we see the whole, the 'gestalt' rather than the segments of the blocks. Similarly, people with autism perform better on embedded figures tasks where a small shape has to be detected inside a larger design.

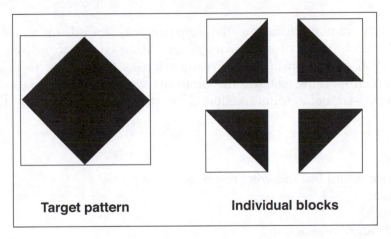

| Target pattern | Individual blocks |

Figure 3.4 Block design sub-test

In memory tasks comparing memory for sentences with memory for unconnected word strings, most of us benefit from the meaning of the sentences and remember them better. However, people with autism remember unconnected strings of words equally well. It seems to be specifically in connecting words or objects that coherence is weak in those with autism (Happe 1994).

Implications of weak central coherence for Early Years practice

- Young children with autism often have an *idiosyncratic focus of attention*. An example of this was seen in a Nursery school where a group of children were sitting with their teacher, singing rhymes. Ricky, aged three, although sitting amongst them, was preoccupied with sniffing the leaf of a nearby plant. On a later visit to the Nursery, Ricky was fully involved in singing time and seemed indistinguishable from the other children. In the meantime, a support assistant had been working with Ricky for 15 to 20 minutes each day, using Musical Interaction techniques to build up his awareness of familiar action rhymes.

- *Imposition of their own perspective* is characteristic of young children with autism – what appears prominent to the child determines his interaction in the learning situation. Mention animals to five year old Liam and he is fully involved, spelling 'dinosaur' and 'rhinoceros' with ease. But given 'in' or 'on' in the spelling test, he becomes distressed and cannot do it. His skills in this area were extended and his anxiety reduced by helping him compose and write sentences about animals which included the words that had worried him in the test. He was particularly motivated if this activity was carried out on the computer.

- Given that young children with autism have a *preference for the known* it was not surprising that when the route into nursery was changed one day because workmen were repairing a burst water pipe Sally screamed inconsolably, unable to accept the change.
- Most young children with autism have *difficulties choosing*. Amina is fine at Nursery when the activities are well structured, but finds 'choosing time' very difficult. She appears agitated, starts to hum and spin round and round. Nursery staff realise that they need to specifically teach her how to make choices. At first limiting the items on offer to just two – one that they know she likes and one that she is usually not interested in, is helping to make the choice clear.

Executive function

Among alternative explanations for the impairments found in autism is that proposed by Ozonoff (1995) of a disorder of executive control functions. Ozonoff quotes Luria's 1966 definition of executive function as 'the ability to maintain an appropriate problem-solving set for the attainment of a future goal'. Executive function encompasses behaviours mediated by the frontal lobes of the brain, including:

- planning;
- impulse control;
- inhibition of prepotent but incorrect responses;
- set maintenance;
- organised search;
- flexibility of thought and action.

Russell *et al.* (1999) define the two main components of an executive function task. The participant has to:

1. suppress a prepotent but incorrect response;
2. retain action-relevant information while doing so.

The following examples illustrate how prepotent (or dominant) responses can interfere with learning tasks.

- Jack was asked to name the colours of the pans in the home corner at his nursery. The teacher pointed to the red one and he said, 'red', she pointed to the green one and he said, 'green', but when she pointed to the blue one he replied, 'Thomas'. He was unable to suppress his inclination to relate all blue things to Thomas the Tank Engine.
- Naomi was doing a matching task in her Reception class which involved using coins and pictures. She successfully named each coin and matched it to its picture. When the task altered and she was asked to 'Give me' a particular coin Naomi started to line up and spin the coins, unable to inhibit her preferred way of using the materials.

Temple Grandin (1995), an extremely able person with autism, supports the notion of an executive function in autism, saying, 'I cannot hold one piece of information in my mind while I manipulate the next step in the sequence'.

Executive function deficits have been proposed to explain many of the experimental findings in autism. Russell *et al.* (1999) contend that difficulties with 'theory of mind' tasks can be explained by difficulties with the executive structure of the tasks. Ozonoff *et al.* (1991), finding that people with autism confuse fear and surprise when looking at an open mouthed expression, suggest that this is due to an inability to retain a model of the emotional image. Other researchers have suggested that imitation difficulties stem from an inability to retain a mental model of the action to be copied, and that pretend play deficits arise from a similar problem – that is, in responding to external rather than internal cues.

However, it is argued that executive function deficits cannot offer a satisfactory explanation of the specific deficits of autism, since executive function deficits also occur in other conditions, e.g. Attention Deficit Disorder, without autism being present (Bishop 1993). Executive functioning deficit may therefore be, a necessary, but not sufficient, condition of autism (Jordan 1999).

Implications of executive function deficits for Early Years practice

An awareness of the possible effects of executive function deficits points us in the direction of intervention.

- In order to enhance the child's *perception and recognition of emotional expression* it is important to exaggerate, prolong and emphasise facial expressions, gestures and body language.
- In order to enhance *imitation skills* we will need to find ways of drawing the child's attention to the model to be imitated, using exaggeration, musical clues and visual cues. Multi-sensory approaches will be necessary. Elroy had learned to recognise a sad face in a picture. After he'd fallen over and hurt himself he went over to the classroom mirror to check his facial expression to see how sad he was. He had learned to recognise the outer appearance of sadness rather than the inner feeling.
- In attempting to elicit *pretend play* we will need to start from reality based routines and include stimulating props, music, story sacks and familiar rhymes. At the Child Development Centre, the teacher would act out simple stories dramatically, using props to illustrate each element. Telling 'Mrs Wishy Washy' would involve dressing up in a headscarf and apron, using a tray of soil for the toy animals to get dirty in, and a washing up bowl of soapy water and scrubbing brush to clean them with. Ryan and Tim, both four years of age, once familiar with the story, would dress up and act it out themselves.
- The *planning and organisation skills* of the young child with autism can be developed through the use of visual or concrete sequences, e.g. pictures or objects of reference, which also emphasise starting and end points.
- Finally, we can take care to alter the environmental stimuli which may serve as triggers to difficult behaviour.

In terms of learning to learn skills it will be useful to:

- break tasks down into clearly identifiable steps;
- develop a hierarchy of sub-goals;
- sequence activities towards the goals;
- identify the main idea in new information;
- make associations between new learning tasks and previously acquired skills explicit.

Summary

As Jordan (1999) points out, 'There is as yet no one commanding theory to explain the cause of autism.' However, each contributes something to our understanding of the processes.

- The impairments revealed in 'theory of mind' investigations highlight the difficulty people with autism have in understanding others' mental states.

- Intersubjectivity theories emphasize the difficulties with emotional understanding and underline the importance of emotional involvement in learning.
- The central coherence deficit theory indicates the importance of ensuring the appropriate focus of attention and catering for a particular learning style.
- Suggested difficulties in developing an 'experiencing self' indicate the need for teaching approaches designed to enhance self-awareness and personal memory.
- Theories of executive function deficit confirm the necessity for structure and clarity in teaching approaches.

As Jordan comments, 'good practice implications, in terms of teaching content and approach, can be derived from a number of contrasting theoretical understandings'. Different theoretical understandings can nevertheless result in similar teaching approaches.

4 | Intervention approaches

In recent years, alongside the burgeoning range of theories to explain autism, there has been a dramatic increase in the number and range of intervention approaches proposed. Some of these approaches have been specifically designed with autism in mind, while others are adaptations of approaches found to help children and adults with a variety of other difficulties.

Each approach stems from a particular understanding of autism, its nature and causes, and aims to develop a way of compensating for the perceived deficit or enhancing the perceived strengths.

For instance some approaches start with an understanding that autism is a biological difficulty. The perceived factors responsible for causing or contributing to autism are organic brain dysfunction, epilepsy, hearing and/or visual difficulties. This may then direct the focus of intervention towards the pharmacological or dietary, e.g. *Opioid Excess Theory*.

Another group of approaches starts from a behavioural background which is based on the notion that all behaviour is learned and can be altered by shaping, then rewarding desired behaviours, e.g. *Applied Behavioural Analysis* (Lovaas).

Many different approaches have been found to be effective in improving the ability of individual children to make sense of the world in which they live. However, no *single* approach has yet been found which is effective with *all* children with autism. Moreover, individual approaches improve the functioning of children with autism, but no approach can be seen as a cure.

Elizabeth Newson (1979) believes it is important to address 'the whole nature of autism'. She feels that as long as interventions concentrate on a single aspect of the condition, they miss the point that 'every kind of impairment in autism has links with every other impairment in the syndrome. They all overflow into and pervade each other and it is indeed the interaction between the different parts of the syndrome which is most characteristic of autism.' A combination of elements from different approaches might, therefore, be the most effective intervention, see Figure 4.1.

The following is a compilation of a number of current approaches. It aims to give a brief overview of each approach, looking at the main elements, the theoretical background, what happens in the approach, and the approach's application to autism together with an evaluation.

In the authors' own work with young children with autism we have found some of these approaches extremely productive. Among these are *TEACCH*, *PECS* and *Musical Interaction*.

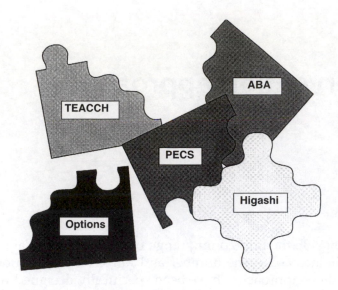

Figure 4.1 A combination of intervention approaches can be effective

TEACCH (Treatment and Education of Autistic and related Communication handicapped CHildren)

TEACCH is a whole life approach to helping people with autism, which aims to equip children for a productive life in the community. It sets out to provide visual information, structure and predictability as it is recognised that the optimum learning channel is visual.

It began in 1966 in North Carolina as a research project which was funded by the Federal US Government. The project, led by Eric Schopler and colleagues, developed from clinical experience at the University of North Carolina. It was established in 1972 as a state-wide programme. Since its foundation, Division TEACCH has worked with some 4,000 people with autism in North Carolina and has developed over the years in many parts of the world.

The University of North Carolina continues to be at the core, offering services and opportunities for training and research, allowing easy access for clinicians and families to the latest developments. There is a comprehensive and integrated service for families, which facilitates access to assessment and intervention.

The approach requires that adaptations must occur in the three major areas of the child's life: home, school and community. Starting with a comprehensive assessment the approach comprises a number of interconnected elements, which are based on structured teaching.

Structured teaching

Physical structure

This refers to the way in which the environment is organised. There are clear visual boundaries segmenting the space into recognisable parts. This helps the children understand what they are expected to do in each area. In the area set aside for work, distractions are kept to a minimum.

The schedule

This tells the child visually what activities will occur and in which order. Using objects, photos, pictures, numbers or words (depending on the individual's developmental level) the child is helped to understand a sequence of events.

Work systems

Through these systems the child is taught:

- What task/activity do I have to do?
- How much do I have to do?
- When will I have finished?
- What will I have to do next?

Visual clarity

Tasks are presented visually so as to make the expectations clear and highlight the important information.

Theoretical background

In the 1960s the prevailing approach to autism was psychotherapy. Children with autism were considered to be ineducable and were often removed from their parents. Schopler and Reichler worked with many children with autism and their families. The experience led them to believe that autism stemmed from some form of brain abnormality, rather than from 'refrigerator' parenting.

They believed that the best way forward was to work with parents, helping them to develop skills and understanding, so that parents became co-therapists. They understood that children with autism found the world a confusing, unpredictable and sometimes frightening place. They were also aware that these children were relatively good visual learners. This led to the development of visual structure and teaching strategies to help the children and young people make sense of the world and what was expected of them.

? What happens?

In North Carolina, access to TEACCH starts with a diagnostic assessment, which is followed by the development of behaviour management techniques and the planning of a home teaching programme.

As the child moves into the education system, continuous assessment takes place using the Psycho-Educational Profile – Revised (PEP-R). This identifies what the child knows and identifies the next areas of learning. A programme is designed in which new skills are taught in a one to one situation with the teacher; current skills are practised in an independent situation; and opportunities for social interaction take place in group activities.

Adolescent and adult services develop respite programmes, vocational training, social skills training groups, job advocacy and facilitate integration into the world of work.

Staff training is considered an important element with each staff member receiving 5–10 in-service training activities each year. Through this system skills are increased, enhancing the application of the programme. It also helps to reduce stress and burnout.

In the UK, TEACCH strategies are used in most specialist schools for children with autism, and they have also been found useful in supporting children in mainstream schools and early years settings. The following are examples of how TEACCH principles have been successfully used with young children with autism.

- Ella, aged three, used to scream every time her Mummy wanted to take her out in the car, but she would calm down once they arrived at their destination. A collection of visual and tactile cues was assembled, each to indicate a possible place to be visited. These included a photograph of Grandma, a supermarket carrier bag and an empty Macdonald's drink carton. Once shown these prior to getting in the car, Ella could predict where she was being taken and no longer screamed.

- Kyle, aged four in a Nursery class, made a beeline for the train-set every day, showing little interest in anything else. A picture timetable was used to prompt him to try other activities – alternating with playing with the trains.
- Jordan, aged five in a Reception class at a special school for children with moderate learning difficulties, was very distractible. He found it particularly difficult to focus on his work when sitting around a table with other children. His teacher arranged a distraction free table at one side of the classroom, facing a plain display screen. Each task he had to do was in its own basket. For short periods of time each day, he followed a simple, colour-coded picture timetable as he worked through each task. Through this strategy, Jordan was much more able to concentrate than he had been before. He also needed less adult prompting and worked more independently.

Application to autism

TEACCH, whilst not addressing autism directly, provides what might be called a 'prosthetic environment' whereby many of the difficulties can be circumvented and people with autism can be enabled to live and learn without undue stress and anxiety.

Central to TEACCH is a system of structured teaching, which maximises the visual presentation and minimises verbal instruction. This structure aims to make use of the strengths of children with autism, their visual skills and adherence to routine, and use these strengths to help minimise their difficulties.

The structured teaching approach helps children and young people with autism make sense of their surroundings and what is expected of them. This has the effect of reducing the frustration and anxiety, which could, in less structured circumstances, lead to behaviour problems. It helps them to move towards independent working and is suitable for use across the age and ability range.

Evaluation

Significant improvement in appropriate behaviour and communication are the main reported benefits. The structure helps children to focus appropriately on tasks without anxiety, which, in turn, facilitates access to the curriculum.

Some feel that TEACCH over-structures children, limiting their decision making and creativity. But flexibility is encouraged within the structured framework, particularly in developing problem-solving skills.

TEACCH focuses on the individual child and his/her strengths. The predictability of the environment minimises anxieties, and maximises attention to the task.

For further information, contact: Division TEACCH, CB#7180, Medical School Wing E, University of North Carolina, Chapel Hill, NC 27599, USA.
Telephone: +(919) 966 2173
Fax: +(919) 966 4127

Intensive interaction

Intensive interaction was developed as an approach to teaching people with severe learning disabilities. It aims to develop and extend basic social and communication skills. The approach was developed by Melanie Nind and David Hewett and (1994), in their work at Harperbury Hospital School. Their client group included young people with challenging behaviours, some of whom had autism.

Theoretical background

The approach is based on the model of caregiver–infant interaction. It begins by imitating the model of early learning in which the young child and the caregiver build up an interactive relationship. For the majority of young children the first eighteen months of life are spent learning about sociability and communication. The most important aspect of this is mutual enjoyment, encouraging the child to enjoy being with the adult and vice-versa.

? What happens?

There are regular, frequent interactions between the practitioner and the child in which there is no task or outcome focus, but in which the primary concern is for the quality of the interaction itself. The actions of the child or adult with autism are imitated and incorporated into turn-taking routines with the teacher. Thus, a repertoire of playful routines is developed which is based on activities which are enjoyable to the child/adult. In this way a relationship is built up that can be used to assist learning in all areas. The practitioner has the role of scaffolding the experience so that it is safe by being familiar, but stimulating in that it extends the child's skills of communication and increases their level of sociability.

The following is an example of the technique in use with a young child with autism:

- In the Child Development Centre Max, aged two and a half, was like 'a little boy lost'. He was perplexed by the adults and children around him, and spent much of his time frowning and walking up and down in a straight line. He was more relaxed in the soft-play room – particularly if no other children were there. The teacher played alongside him, echoing each of his rare vocalisations, leaving gaps for him to repeat his own sound. In time, a very basic turn-taking dialogue developed. The teacher went on to introduce a simple game involving sounds and actions. Saying, 'up, up, up' as she lifted her arms above her head, then pausing before saying 'down' as she brought her hands down to tickle Max. He giggled at the tickling and soon learnt to anticipate when the tickle would come. He began to prompt a repeat of the game by touching the teacher's hand, by looking towards her, and sometimes, by vocalising.

Application to autism

The authors recognise that the Triad of Impairments associated with autism pose a massive challenge in the development of social and communication skills.

The emphasis is on getting to know the individual with autism, following his lead and giving him time. In this way there is an increase in the positive attitudes of both parties to initiate and respond to the interactions. Nind and Hewett talk of the children with autism becoming more 'available'.

Evaluation

The approach is non-confrontational and follows the child's lead at his/her own pace, an aspect that is seen as positive. Hewett and Nind (1998) give examples of the progress made by children when this approach is used. They note an increase in sociability, communication and responsiveness in children with autism who were previously regarded as 'hard to reach'. Parents, by being encouraged to follow their intuition, are also empowered in their dealings with their child.

Intensive interaction should be seen as one element in a package of intervention strategies within the Early Years curriculum. It is a strategy which makes a particular contribution to the development of basic communication skills.

For further information, contact Melanine Nind, at the Open University at Milton Keynes.

Musical interaction

The aim of musical interaction is to engage each child in the process of interaction, to build up the desire for communication rather than it becoming a mechanical response to adult expectations. This approach is based on the caregiver–child interaction, on the way that parents naturally play with young children. The emphasis is on helping the child to develop communicative intent. It focuses on what the child can do and builds on this. In this way it shares the same root as Intensive interaction, with the additional factor of music to facilitate and reinforce communication and the child's role in the process.

Theoretical background

The approach is based on the observations of early interaction between caregivers and very young children. In a normally developing child there is a strong motivation to communicate. It is a two-way process fostered by mutual enjoyment. In this approach the adult is encouraged to highlight the interaction with music which may originate with the voice or an instrument/s.

What happens?

At first the adult responds to the child's spontaneous sounds and movements as if they are intentionally communicative; this may encourage the child to start using them intentionally. Prevezer (1990) pinpoints ways of 'tuning in' to the child. She begins by creating shared attention, by joining in with or imitating the child. She then gives a simple running commentary to the child's actions, which is spoken, chanted, sung or played on an instrument. Use of songs, rhymes and play routines as frameworks for communication, creating pauses for anticipation, helps to underscore the interaction.

The following is an example of the approach being used with a young child with autism:

- Ricky, aged three, attended a Nursery. He found it difficult to cope with 'singing time' amongst a group of children. A support assistant spent time with him each day, introducing one song at a time to him. She began with songs that had actions, as these seemed to grab his attention more than the words. She would repeat a song a few times, and then begin to pause towards the end of a line before singing the final word or phrase. Soon Ricky began to supply the missing words himself. He also started to prompt the support assistant to repeat favourite songs by spontaneously singing the first few words and waiting for her to join in.

Application to autism

This approach was devised at a local Autistic Society school, and was specifically aimed at children with autism attending the school. (Christie *et al.* 1992, Prevezer 1990, Wimpory *et al.* 1995). It was recognised that children with autism appear to lack the basic motivation to interact, and felt that they were likely to have missed out on the early interactive stages of social development. By teaching the skills of communication in an interactive way the practitioner hopes to facilitate an enjoyment of being in an interactive process. For many children with autism the control is in the hands of the non-autistic person and they are expected to follow their example. In this approach control is shared between the two partners.

 Evaluation

Musical intraction is a non-invasive approach which encourages valuing the child and valuing the interaction that takes place. This encourages a more positive view of the child by those who live and work with him. It gives permission to the adult to follow the child's lead and to interact with the child at the developmental level rather than the age level.

Some teachers fear that they need to be music specialists in order to use this approach. However, this is not the case. None of the authors could be described as musical, but all have successfully used this approach.

For further information, contact: The Early Years Centre, 272 Longdale Lane, Ravenshead, Nottingham. NG15 9AH. *Telephone*: 01623 490879

Picture Exchange Communication System (PECS)

PECS was developed over ten years ago in the USA by Andrew Bondy and Lori Frost within the Delaware Autistic Programme in the USA. It is now also used in Britain with children with Autistic Spectrum Disorders. The aim of PECS is for children to acquire key communication skills especially initiating communication in a social exchange (Bondy 1996).

Theoretical background

Observations of preschool children admitted to the Delaware Programme showed that 80 per cent of children with autism at five years and younger did not have any useful speech (Bondy and Frost 1995). Some other approaches aimed at developing communication can often be slow to acquire and may not lead to functional communication at all. By using reinforcers to motivate communication it has been found that PECS offers an opportunity to quickly develop 'real', spontaneous communication.

? What happens?

Initially two adults are needed. PECS starts by establishing the greatest motivator for the child: this may be food, drink, a toy or an activity – a symbol card is made to represent this. One adult shows the motivator to the child. As the child reaches for it, the second adult assists the child to pick up the symbol card and put it into the hand of the other adult. No verbal prompts are used but lots of praise is given when the child gives the card – and the child receives the motivator. After several exchanges the child begins to initiate the interaction.

As the child becomes at ease with the system other symbols are added, including sentence words like, 'I want...' and the second adult moves further away so that the child has to make a greater effort to get what he wants.

The following is an example of the approach being used with a young child with autism:

- Emily, aged three, was receiving weekly Portage home visits. She showed many signs of frustration, often flying into a tantrum for no obvious reason. Emily had no speech, and her vocalisation wasn't used communicatively. She never initiated an interaction with her Mummy.

  PECS was introduced to Emily via brief, daily Portage visits over a three-week period. She very quickly got the idea, and for the first time was able to initiate communication. Her symbol vocabulary increased rapidly and her frustration diminished, as she was able to explain what she wanted. In addition, she began to develop communicative use of gesture, touching and vocalisation in order to attract her Mummy's attention before giving her the PECS card.

Application to autism

This approach was specifically developed with the needs of young children with autism in mind. It was recognised that these children require highly structured intervention to develop the language and social skills needed for communication. PECS aims to establish the basic skills of communication perhaps even before words are understood or uttered.

Evaluation

In Schools and Units that use PECS within a structured learning environment improvement in communication has been noted. It would appear that a result of using the symbol cards before words is that language becomes more accessible and many of the children have gone on to develop spontaneous speech. As the confidence in communication has grown there has been a noticeable decrease in frustration.

For further information, contact: Pyramid Educational Consultants UK Ltd, 17 Prince Albert Street, Brighton BN1 1HF. *Telephone:* 01273 728888

SPELL (The National Autistic Society (NAS) approach to autism)

It was recognised within NAS schools that in order to address the triad of impairments, there needed to be a distinctly different teaching style. The acronym that describes the approach that was put together is SPELL.

Theoretical background

The NAS set up its first school in 1964, and now runs 13 schools. The work within these establishments has concentrated on specific programmes to reduce the effects of the triad of impairments. These programmes have recognised that structure, consistency, reduction of disturbing stimuli and a high degree of organisation offer the optimum environment for learning to take place.

What happens?

It is essential that children are taught in appropriately organised and supported settings. The teachers within schools plan curriculum delivery so that the child is able to predict events and so reduce anxiety.

The approach draws on elements from a number of other approaches, combining them flexibly with the aim of meeting individual needs.

Application to autism

This approach is a response to the triad of impairments. SPELL stands for:

Structure – by giving the day a recognisable structure the child feels more secure.

Positive approaches and expectations to enhance the child's self-confidence and self-esteem.

Empathy – the teacher designs a differentiated programme that takes on the individual child's needs.

Low arousal settings so that the child is not distracted or made over anxious by the environment. There are also planned periods of physical education and/or relaxation.

Links with parents, schools, other agencies and the wider community.

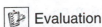 Evaluation

As yet there has been no formal evaluation of SPELL, but the NAS is following up the children and adults against a baseline assessment.

For further information, contact: The Director of Services, The National Autistic Society, Church House, Church Road, Filton, Bristol BS12 7BD. *Fax:* 0117 987 2576
Or contact: NAS Training, Castle Heights, 4th Floor, 72 Maid Marion Way, Nottingham NG1 6BJ. *Telephone:* 0115 911 3360 *Fax:* 0115 911 2259

The Earlybird project

The National Autistic Society (NAS) initially set up the Earlybird project in Barnsley to help parents understand autism and how it affects their child. The project is managed by speech and language therapist Dr Jane Shields.

Theoretical background

The NAS has always been committed to work with parents of children with autism. Through this work it has recognised that structured intervention, offered as soon as possible after diagnosis, is extremely beneficial for children with autism (Peacock *et al.* 1996). It has also recognised that the involvement of parents in early intervention has a positive influence on the outcomes (Guralnick 1997, Rossetti 1996).

The programme aims to:

- put parents in control to develop the potential of their child;
- empower parents, and help them facilitate their child's social communication and appropriate behaviour within the child's natural environment;
- support parents in the period between diagnosis and school placement;
- assist parents in establishing good practice in managing their child at an early age, preventing the development of inappropriate behaviours.

? What happens?

The project accepts families whose preschool child has a diagnosis of an autistic spectrum disorder and who live within easy travelling distance of the base. Groups of six families at a time join for a 12-week programme. This involves daytime training sessions for carers, interspersed with home visits to provide individualised help for each family to help them put theory into practice.

The programme incorporates aspects of the Hanen Program for early language intervention, which has been modified for children with autism, together with aspects of TEACCH, and the use of reinforcers.

⊕ Application to autism

The approach is founded on current understanding of autism based on work undertaken within the NAS. Accordingly the programme is a response to the demands of the triad of impairments. Thus the programme aims to increase the child's desire to communicate and provides the language with which to communicate. It also aims to help prevent the development of asocial behaviours.

📖 Evaluation

At present, Earlybirds is undergoing formal assessment. Anecdotal evidence suggests that parents have increased confidence, the children have increased communicative skills and fewer challenging behaviours.

For further information, contact: NAS Earlybirds Centre, 3 Victoria Crescent West, Barnsley, South Yorkshire, S75 2AE. *Telephone:* 01226 779218 *Fax:* 01226 771014 E-mail: earlybird@dial.pipex.com

Applied Behavioural Analysis (Lovaas)

Behavioural methods have been used in the education of children with autism and severe learning difficulties in the UK for many years.

In the Young Autism Project (1970–84), based in the USA, Lovaas and his colleagues used behavioural techniques with a group of 59 children with autism. The techniques were taught to parents in an intensive home-treatment programme. Lovaas recommends that treatment should begin as early as possible and ideally before the child is 42 months old.

📖 Theoretical background

A behavioural approach is based on the theory that all behaviour is learned and that it is governed by its antecedents and consequences. This is based on Skinner's theory of 'operant conditioning' which was proposed in the 1960s. The foundations of this are that learning can be reduced to the repetition of responses, which increase with reward. In this way a task to be learned can be analysed into small steps which are then used as a teaching programme for the child. Each step can be shaped through positive reinforcement.

In order to count as a behavioural programme there must be:

- periodic and objective assessment;
- reinforcement;
- skilled staff.

? What happens?

It is an intensive intervention, which takes place for up to 40 hours a week for approximately two years. In order to work, it has to be delivered by all the significant persons who work with the child. There is a hierarchy of deliverers including a consultant, a supervisor, and a number of tutors, parents and peers.

Lovaas suggests the following format to the approach:

1. Establish rapport.
2. Extend receptive language, using highly structured speech.
3. Develop imitation skills – non-verbal body imitation.
4. Develop imitation of toy play.
5. Develop verbal imitation.

At an initial consultation the child's baseline skills are identified, and a programme is devised. The programme involves a system of discrete trials in which positive responses are reinforced. New skills are shaped through prompting and chaining. The results are recorded in the logbook to inform future input.

Application to autism

Although ABA was not specifically developed with children with autism in mind, Lovaas felt that it would benefit this group of children. In his view, autism is caused by an abnormal nervous system, which prevents the child learning from the normal environment. Thus if the learning environment is changed then the child can learn.

Lovaas talked of autism being a series of deficits and excesses. The deficits are such behaviours as: poor eye contact, lack of empathy, poor self-help skills. The excesses include: tantrums, stereotypies, obsessive behaviours. The approach is based on building on the deficits and reducing the excesses.

Evaluation

In the Young Autism Project reported by Lovaas in 1987 the results were based on the educational placement and it was found that of the 19 children who had received 40 hours a week input, nine had a normal level of functioning at around seven years of age. In the groups that had less input one out of forty showed a normal level of functioning. At the second follow-up eight out of the original nine were classified as 'indistinguishable from the normal control group'.

At Brunel University the Parents for Early intervention of Autism in Children (PEACH) is replicating the work of the Young Autism Project in order to evaluate the approach.

Behavioural approaches have been criticised for their inappropriate and narrow focus. The social interaction element of communication and pragmatic aspects of language separate us from the pigeons of Skinner's original experiments. However, the parents of young children with autism report significant improvements in their child's ability to access the world, after following the approach.

For further information, contact: Parents for the Early Intervention of Autism in Children, PO Box 10836, London SW13 9ZN.
Telephone: 020 8891 0121
Fax: 020 8891 8209
e-mail: peach@brunel.ac.uk
internet: http://www.peach.uk.com
Or contact the Glenne Centre, PO Box 55, Barre, 3195 Horten, Norway.
e-mail: glennes@online.no

Son-Rise Program (Option Approach)

The Option Institute in Massachusetts is run by Kaufmans. They offer parents training in the Son-Rise Program which they then take home with them and work through with their child. The approach was originally developed by them as they worked with their own young son with autism.

The Son-Rise Program is a home-based, child-centred, parent-directed alternative for parents. The aim is to encourage the child to be self-motivating via non-confrontation and unconditional acceptance.

Theoretical background

The basis of this approach is that everyone has an 'option'. The quality of life we lead is down to us. It is our responsibility and no one else's. Our happiness is our choice and no one has the power to make us unhappy.

The Kaufmans believe that, 'the mind (or brain) has the capacity to restore itself to normal functioning, given the conditions for that to occur' (Jordan 1991).

There are two main parts to the approach. The first is to work with the parents to alter their approach to their child. Their changed attitude alters their behaviour towards the child in such a significant way that he himself will change.

The parents' decision to accept the child as he is, is summarised as 'To love is to be happy with'. Once they are positive about their child, then parents can help their child.

? What happens?

Space is created for the child in a room – the 'playroom'. This room is free from the distractions of everyday life and the focus is totally child-centred, providing a safe, secure, positive environment.

Throughout the day a succession of adults (therapists and carers) enter the playroom to be with the child. The approach to the child is one of high energy using the three 'E's' of Excitement, Enthusiasm and Energy. This increases the desire to interact with the adult. The adult follows the child's lead and engages in his activities, including any stereotypies, thus giving them a positive value.

Application to autism

The Option Approach does not involve any theories about the causes of autism. It accepts the linguistic and cognitive difficulties and that these may have a biological basis. The child is seen as coping as best he can with a world that he can neither understand nor control. His obsessional behaviours, or his withdrawal from the social world are his response to his lack of control.

Some schools have developed an interactive, child-centred approach offering choice and letting the child take the lead, based on aspects of the Option approach.

As a heavily child-centred approach it has much in common with Intensive interaction and musical interaction, described earlier in this chapter.

Evaluation

The use of the playroom in which the child is isolated from non-Option trained individuals can cause concern, as it limits the child's access to family life and the wider community.

The quality and quantity of the child's social responsiveness improves. The most impressive factor in this approach is the change in the parents and their growth in confidence when being with their child. The child has more control and begins to make sense of the wider world through the input of the adults.

For further information, contact: The Option Institute and Fellowship, 2080 South Undermountain Road, Sheffield, Mass., 01257-9643 USA.
Telephone: +(413) 229 – 2100
Fax: +(413) 229 0493
e-mail: startup@option.org

Daily Life Therapy (Higashi)

This approach was developed by Dr Kiyo Kitahara in Tokyo in the 1970s. It is based on the belief that the routines and patterns of daily living can be taught through the rhythm of life in the group process. This appears to be based on an eastern philosophy of harmony between the spirit, body and mind. It also takes account of the importance given to the group situation in Japanese culture.

In 1987 the approach forwarded in Daily Life Therapy was transferred to Boston in the USA and it is expected that a similar school will be established in England.

 Theoretical background

Daily Life Therapy is an approach that aims to give the child the necessary skills for daily life, by establishing patterns of acceptable behaviour through stabilising the emotions, establishing a rhythm of life and stimulating the intellect. Dr Kitahara believed that children with autism would benefit from close links with their families and a 'traditional curriculum' in a community of children with a similar cultural experience.

The three elements of the therapy are:

- *stability of emotions*, gained through the development of self-esteem and the pursuit of independent living;
- *improved physical strength*, achieved through the development of motor co-ordination, stamina and strength;
- *stimulation of the intellect*, in the areas of language, arts, maths and social sciences.

| ? | What happens?

In the school situation the children are taught in groups. Staff:child ratios vary from 1:5 to 1:3, with one adult leading the group and the other adult/s prompting the children's input from behind. Verbal instructions are kept short, clear and concise and no alternative forms of communication are used or taught. Activities are all group orientated and highly structured with all children being expected to learn through imitation and synchronised activities. The activity progresses at the rate of the slowest child.

The curriculum consists of language, arts, maths and social sciences with PE being the strongest curriculum subject. There is great emphasis on physical activity with a number of periods each day being allotted to strenuous physical exercise. Festivals and displays are part of the curriculum.

Application to autism

Dr Kitahara recognised that children with autism are socially isolated, developmentally delayed and often anxious. Daily Life Therapy is a holistic approach which aims to reduce the child's autism by developing close bonds in the family, with the teachers and between the children in the group who are kept together. The high level of physical exercise has been found to be beneficial to all children with autism.

Evaluation

In the 1960s Dr Kitahara established the Musashino Higashi Gakuen School in Tokyo, a specialised school in which children with autism could be included with 'normal' children for group education.

In 1987 the International Boston Higashi School was opened. The difference between the Japanese school and the US school is that in the US the school is attended exclusively by children who have an Autistic Spectrum Disorder. The children are drawn from a large catchment area, including overseas. This reduces opportunities for family input and for integration into schools in the child's home locality.

Parents report great improvement in self-help skills such as toileting and feeding, including a wider tolerance of foods. The predictability of the rhythm seems to foster a sense of calmness in the children. There is high achievement in the areas of PE and music, which can result in an increased level of self-esteem and confidence.

From the personal experience of one of the authors, having worked with a child on return from Higashi, it would seem that the claimed reduction of stereotypical behaviours is difficult to maintain once the child has left the specialist environment. Higashi has also been criticised on the basis of what seems to be a relatively narrow curriculum – much narrower than the National Curriculum. Underfunctioning can also be a problem, as the individuality of different ability levels is not catered for.

For further information, contact: Robert A. Fantasia, Principal Director of Special Education, 800 North Main Street, Rudolph, Mass., 02368, USA.
Or contact Mrs Rita Murray, 71 Heath Park Road, Romford, Essex, RM2 5UL.

Auditory Integration Training (AIT)

The Auditory Integration Training technique was originally used to treat hypersensitive hearing, deafness and other hearing problems. It was developed by two French physicians, Alfred Tomatis and Guy Berard. The methods used by Tomatis and Berard are similar, but not identical. They share the same basic method, which involves playing electronically filtered music to the patient via headphones. The theory is that it will help to correct hearing distortions and other factors such as dyslexia, attention deficit, hyperactivity, depression and autism.

AIT requires the child to listen to electronically processed music through headphones for a total of 10 hours, usually in two 30-minute sessions, over a 10-day period. The Tomatis Approach involves treatment of approximately 150 hours of treatment over several months.

Theoretical background

Dr Berard was an experienced ear, nose and throat specialist and when he himself began to go deaf he had the idea that he could make a machine that would exercise the entire hearing apparatus. He called this machine the 'Audiokinetron'. He believed that hearing disorders could be helped by auditory exercise the same way that muscular problems can be treated by physical exercise.

What happens?

The AIT technique involves taking two or three audiograms. The first audiogram is taken at the start of the treatment to identify which are the areas of hypersensitivity. The music is filtered in two ways, randomly and stop band. The random filtering is to exercise the hearing. The stop band filtering removes any frequency at which sensitivity occurs. This is to stop the ear becoming 'lazy' to these frequencies resulting in a normalisation of hearing.

A final audiogram is taken at the end of the treatment to check the success of the treatment. Where the treatment has been successful the audiogram should reveal normalisation of hearing.

✜ Application to autism

The use of this technique for children with autism was publicised by Annabel Stehli in her book, *The Sound of a Miracle* (Stehli 1992). In the book, she describes the experience of her daughter Georgiana when she received AIT from Guy Berard in France and how she was 'cured' by AIT.

Tomatis and Berard differ in their view of the nature of autism. Tomatis considers autism to be psychogenic in nature and Berard believes that hearing problems contribute to the behaviours often seen in a person with autism.

✐ Evaluation

Many parents mention the cost of the treatment as being high. Some parents report increased calmness, reduced aggression and a sharp reduction in problem behaviours, while other parents report increased hyperactivity and increased tantrums.

Guy Berard doesn't consider AIT a cure for autism but considers many people will benefit from the treatment.

For further information, contact: Auditory Integration Training, The Light and Sound Therapy Centre, 90 Queen Elizabeth's Walk, London N16 5UQ.
Telephone: 020 8880 1269
Or contact Tomatis Centre UK Ltd, 3 Wallends Crescent, Lewes, East Sussex BN7 2QT.
Tel: 01273 474877
Fax: 01273 487500

Diet (Opioid Excess Theory)

Many parents report that their child has certain intolerances to a variety of foods while others have recorded how eating certain food has resulted in an increase in negative behaviours. Dr Paul Shattock at the Autism Research Unit at the University of Sunderland has undertaken a study of the effects of diet on the autistic population.

📖 Theoretical background

Food tolerance is a major issue across the whole population. There are a number of metabolic disorders, which can result in problems with the digestion of foods. During digestion proteins consisting of thousands of amino acids in a chain are broken down. This process involves the temporary production of peptides, which are incompletely digested proteins.

These peptides can have an opioid activity, which is a morphine-like compound or 'exorphin'. The peptides should remain in the intestine until they are further broken down. However, if for whatever reason they cross the intestine wall and enter the bloodstream they will reach the central nervous system and affect transmission in all systems of the brain. Exorphins can act as 'ligands' for the enzymes which would break down our naturally produced opioid peptides (endomorphines) so that they persist much longer than they should and similarly affect the systems of the brain.

? What happens?

A child may be given an 'exclusion' diet to identify which foods are the cause of the problem. Once the foods have been identified they are excluded from the diet. The most often reported offenders are foods that include gluten, the protein from wheat and certain other cereals, and casein, the protein from milk.

Application to autism

An excess of urinary peptides has been found in 85–90 per cent of examined cases of autistic syndromes (Shattock 1990). This led to the suggestion that toxicity may result in, or magnify the symptoms of autism. The areas that may be affected are: an impaired immune system, perception, cognition, learning and understanding, motivation, stereotypies and boredom.

Many children with autism have bowel problems; either constipation or diarrhoea may result. This could be a consequence of opioid peptides, which will affect the intestines, or allergies to gluten or milk. There has also been some suggestion that there may be evidence of lingering measles infections in the intestines of some children with autism.

 Evaluation

There is anecdotal evidence from parents that the restriction diet has had major benefits for children who have autism. The children are reported to be more attentive, more willing to interact and calmer. Norwegian observers have been following the same cohort of children for seven years. Their observations tend to correspond to the parental reports.

Some families find it difficult to follow a very restricted diet. One parent commented that her child appeared to have so little pleasure that to take away favourite foods as well was not fair. Others report very little change in the child's behaviour.

Paul Shattock reports that not all people with autism benefit from the diet. It seems that, 'younger, more seriously afflicted children respond more dramatically than older people whose difficulties are less severe'.

For further information, contact: The Autism Research Unit, The School of Health Sciences, University of Sunderland, Sunderland SR2 7EE.
Tel: 0191 510 8922
Fax: 0191 567 0420

Secretin

Secretin is a neurotransmitter in the neuropeptide group. It is one of the hormones naturally present in the pancreas, and a deficiency of secretin is meant to suggest a digestive problem. It is used to test for gastrointestinal problems as an injection of secretin stimulates the production of the digestive fluids, pepsin and bile.

Theoretical background

While using secretin for digestive investigations in some children, behavioural changes were observed. As outlined in 'Opioid Excess Theory', problems with digestion can lead to peptides crossing through the gut and affecting the nervous system. Secretin stimulates the pancreas to produce the enzymes that break down the peptides and so reduce the problems caused by these peptides.

? What happens?

Children are given a series of injections of secretin.

⬙ Application to autism

As outlined earlier in 'Opioid Excess Theory' many children have digestive problems resulting in either constipation or diarrhoea.

The increasing use of secretin as a treatment for children with autism was prompted by the experience of the Beck family in the USA. Parker Beck, a young boy with autism, who suffered with constant diarrhoea and vomiting, was taken into hospital for an endoscopy. Part of the procedure was an injection of secretin. A few days after the procedure Parker's diarrhoea disappeared, he started to sleep through the night for the first time and he began to talk.

⬙ Evaluation

Secretin has not been approved for the treatment of autism. The concern is that no one knows what are the side effects of long term use of secretin. Trials are being undertaken in the USA which should give a clearer indication of the effectiveness of secretin.

Not all children who have tried secretin have shown the increase in skills that seemed to be present in Parker Beck. These injections are costly and some adverse effects are reported.

For further information, contact: The Autism Research Unit, The School of Health Sciences, University of Sunderland, Sunderland SR2 7EE.
Telelphone:0191 510 8922
Fax: 0191 567 0420

Irlen

The Irlen Institute has been studying the use of tinted lenses with people with learning disabilities since 1981. Helen Irlen, founder of the Institute, discovered that viewing the written word through different coloured overlays seemed to help a certain group of children with reading difficulties or Scotopic Sensitivity Syndrome (SSS). These children had adequate decoding skills, good phonetic skills and adequate sight vocabulary. It appeared that their problem was in perceiving words on a page. They were perceiving words in a distorted way as a result of a sensitivity to certain wavelengths of light.

The Irlen treatment uses coloured filters worn as glasses to reduce or eliminate perceptual difficulties. The colour appears to change the rate at which the brain processes information.

⬙ Theoretical background

Seventy per cent of the information an individual receives comes through the eyes and must be correctly interpreted by the brain. Distortion of the words on the page is a perceptual difficulty. Extending the understanding of the impact of these perceptual problems and their effect on the senses and how they process information forms the basis of this approach.

⬙ What happens?

The person is screened to see if he can benefit from the use of coloured lenses. Different coloured lenses are experimented with until an optimum clarity is reached. Then this individual combination of the coloured discs is put together to tint the lenses of the person's glasses.

Donna Williams (1998) in her autobiography, *Like Colour to the Blind*, describes the impact a visit to the Irlen Centre had on her and her friend Ian. Once she had found the best tint and was wearing the glasses, she found that she was able to listen and concentrate better. In addition, her speech became more fluent and spontaneous, she could understand the words she was reading and was able to integrate fragmented information into the context of her surroundings.

Application to autism

Once Donna Williams had announced to the world the 'miraculous' improvements resulting from wearing her Irlen lenses, other people with autism attended the Institute and claim to have benefited from wearing the lenses. Improvement has been reported in the areas of the integration of sense perceptions, ability to respond, body and spatial awareness, eye contact, communication and self-control.

It has been recognised that 40 per cent (Rimland 1990) of the autistic population have sensory difficulties, and these lead to problems in assimilating information accessed through these senses. Helen Irlen found that all the senses are connected, so that visual perception may affect the processes which influence auditory perception.

Evaluation

Some people with autism display a high degree of tactile defensiveness and cannot bear to wear the glasses. However, for some of this group the benefits of wearing the glasses outweigh their tactile sensitivity. The most striking difference reported has been the calming effect and a new sense of comfort. Most of the wearers felt more grounded and centred, better able to participate in spontaneous conversations.

For further information, contact: Ann Wright, Irlen Centre East, 4 Park Farm Business Centre, Fornham Street, Genevieve, Bury St Edmunds, Suffolk IP28 6EX. *Telephone:* 01284 724301
Fax: 01284 724301

Choosing an approach

Parents often ask 'What's the best intervention approach for my child?' as the media herald a new 'cure' for autism. It can lead to tension between parents and professionals if queries are met with, 'I don't know. I've never heard of that one!', or if parents have decided a certain approach is best for their child and then ask the Local Education Authority to fund it.

The following questions may be helpful when considering a particular approach:

- On which theory of autism is the approach based?
- How long has the approach been in use for children with autism?
- Was the approach specifically developed for use with children with autism?
- Does this approach benefit all children with autism, or is it designed for use with a specific sub-group?
- What does it involve?
- Who is involved in 'delivering' the approach?
- How is the approach introduced to the child?
- Is it invasive to the child?
- What skills does the approach aim to develop?
- Has the approach been evaluated?
- Can the approach be used in conjunction with any other specific approaches? If so, which?

- To what extent will it affect our family's lifestyle?
- How much does it cost?
- Is it home-based or school-based – or can it be used in both situations?
- How will I know if it is successful?
- What happens if it doesn't work?

Summary

Many different approaches have been outlined in this chapter. Some were developed in an attempt to address specific aspects of autism, e.g. communication skills. Others attempt to enhance a range of skills.

While many have been found to be effective in improving the ability of individual children, no *single* approach has yet been found which is effective with *all* children with autism. In the authors' experience, an approach which combines elements from a number of different approaches, and which is flexible enough to take account of individual differences, is likely to be the most effective intervention.

5 Differentiating the Early Years curriculum and developing play

The foundation stage

Introduced in September 2000, the foundation stage of education is for all children from the age of three to the end of the Reception year. For the first time, this important stage of education has been given a distinct identity. It provides a framework for the provision of education across the whole range of Early Years settings. The foundation stage prepares children for learning in Key Stage 1, and is in line with the National Curriculum.

Areas of learning

The curriculum within the foundation stage is organised in six areas of learning:

- personal, social and emotional development
- communication, language and literacy
- mathematical development
- knowledge and understanding of the world
- physical development
- creative development.

Early Learning Goals

In Early Years settings, all children follow a curriculum and participate in activities which help them make good progress towards the Early Learning Goals (DfEE 1999). These goals are organised in the same six areas as the curriculum. By the end of the foundation stage some children will have achieved or even exceeded these goals, whilst others will be working towards some or all of the goals. Full details of the Early Learning Goals are to be found in Appendix 2.

Meeting the needs of young children with autism

Early Years practitioners have a key role in jointly working with parents and carers to identify and respond to the learning needs of all the individual children in their settings. Careful planning, combined with an understanding of the implications of autism, will be required in order to help young children with autism access the Early Years curriculum.

Each of the six areas of learning presents particular challenges for the young child with autism and for the Early Years practitioner working with him or her. In this chapter, we will consider each area of learning and anticipate some of those challenges.

Following the framework of the DfEE Curriculum Guidance (DfEE 2000), we will also outline the key things practitioners need to know about the learning of young children with autism, and examine the implications for planning and teaching.

---

1. Personal, social and emotional development

To give the young child with autism the best opportunities for personal, social and emotional development, practitioners will need to pay particular attention to:

- establishing a relationship with the child based on consistency and predictability, developing the child's trust and confidence;
- carefully planning and structuring opportunities for the child to work alone, with a partner, in small groups and in larger groups;
- planning experiences which will enable the child to make choices and develop independence within the overall framework;
- sensitively supporting the child through activities (s)he finds challenging;
- identifying what rewards are effective in reinforcing appropriate responses;
- helping young children recognise their own feelings and those of the people around them.

Learning	Teaching
Within this area of learning, children find out about who they are and where they fit in. They learn to respect others and develop social competence and emotional well-being.	Early Years practitioners have a crucial role in developing the social competence of the young child with autism.
The young child with autism begins to trust adults who are consistent in their approach and responses.	There may be a need to assign a key worker to the young child with autism in order to maximise consistency.
The child becomes comfortable with a setting which provides consistent routines through which he can begin to anticipate and predict the shape of the day.	Practitioners need to carefully structure activities and routines, giving visual prompts and clues to aid the child's understanding of what is expected of them.
Young children with autism do not develop relationships with peers spontaneously.	Specific social interaction skills need to be taught – using real social situations.

Stepping stones	*Examples of what children do*
The young child with autism may find it hard at first to tolerate the proximity of other children.	Dean would play with the train set – as long as he had it to himself. If other children tried to join in, he moved away.
The child slowly begins to learn by watching others.	Hannah used to stand watching other children playing with dough. Once they had left the activity, she would begin to explore the dough for herself.
The child slowly develops the ability to understand and accept change.	A picture timetable helped Jon understand what was going to happen each day at nursery.

What does the practitioner need to do?

- Take on board what parents/carers tell you about the child's mood, interests and preferences.
- Start by following the child's lead, seeing what interests him, sit alongside him and gradually share the activity.
- Slowly involve one other child in the activity, introduce turn-taking.
- Carefully structure the activity so that each child's role is obvious.
- Note the child's favoured activities for use as potential rewards.
- Specifically teach imitation skills: 'Watch me! Do this!'.
- Extend this by asking the child to copy what another child is doing.
- Give clear visual clues to help prepare the child for new activities.
- Develop an awareness of the things which may upset the child.

---

2. Communication, language and literacy

To give young children with autism the best opportunities to develop skills in communication, language and literacy, practitioners will need to pay particular attention to:

- helping the child to understand what communication is;
- giving the child a range of verbal and non-verbal strategies through which to communicate;
- helping the child to comprehend the verbal and non-verbal communication of others;
- giving the child opportunities to link language with physical movement in action songs and rhymes;
- giving opportunities to link language (spoken and written) with real life experiences;
- helping the child to develop communication skills in social situations.

Learning	Teaching
This area of learning includes speaking and listening, together with communication in its widest sense.	Practitioners need to be clear about when to take the lead in communication, and how to respond to the child.
Communication is involved in all areas of learning within the Early Years curriculum.	When planning activities, the Early Years practitioner will need to be aware of the child's level of communicative competence.
The young child with autism may not understand what communication is, and may have very limited strategies for getting his message across.	Practitioners will need to respond to the child as if he has communicative intent, and equip the child with strategies for communication.

Stepping stones	Examples of what children do
Joint attention may be difficult to establish at first.	At story time, Billy used to wander off – unaware that he should sit and share the story.
The young child with autism may be slow to use and understand gestures such as pointing.	Jenny would stand near the item she wanted reaching for her, but she didn't point at it or attract an adult's attention.
The child's language may echo chunks of adult language. It may not be used with any communicative intent.	Craig would recite whole sequences of language he'd heard on his favourite video.
The child may be slow to understand verbal instructions – particularly ones addressed to the whole class/group.	When the nursery teacher said, 'Blue group come into the story room', Joe carried on playing – until she said, 'Joe come into the story room'.

What does the practitioner need to do?

- Use attention grabbing toys and activities, linking with the child's own interests.
- Introduce stories and action songs, one to one with the child or in a small group – before expecting him to sit with all the others at story/singing time.
- Exaggerate your facial expressions and gestures to emphasise their meaning.
- Specifically teach pointing – starting with a point which touches the desired item, leading to a distant point later. Use other children to help demonstrate pointing.
- Create situations which could prompt the child into using his language communicatively, e.g. 'forgetting' to give him a straw for his milk carton.
- Place yourself between the child and an item he wants (e.g. the next jigsaw piece or the next Lego brick). Encourage him to prompt you to reach the thing he needs.
- Use visual or musical cues to supplement verbal instructions, e.g. playing a particular piece of music to signal 'come and sit on the carpet'.
- In literacy, be aware that the child may learn to decode words quite quickly, but understanding the meaning of the words he reads takes much longer.

3. Mathematical development

To give young children with autism the best opportunities for mathematical development, practitioners will need to pay particular attention to:

- extending what may be an area of relative strength – the ability to recognise and manipulate shapes;
- linking mathematical concepts with real life situations and activities.

Learning	Teaching
Within this area, children learn to match, sort and count.	Practitioners will need to make early mathematical experiences meaningful for the child.
They learn to recognise patterns, make connections and work with numbers, shapes, space and measures.	The child will need to be guided to see connections, and helped to generalise mathematical skills.

Stepping stones	*Examples of what children do*
The young child with autism may have an interest in numbers.	As Andrew walked to nursery with his Mum, he pointed to door numbers asking, 'What's that?'
He may be able to link numerals to certain quantities.	Although Graham had no expressive language, he could look at any number of counters (up to 10) and point to the correct numeral.
Shape puzzles may be a particular favourite.	William could do puzzles upside-down because he was only looking at the shapes of the pieces – not the picture.
The child may be very good at straightforward calculations, but find number problems very difficult.	Tom, aged 6, could easily solve $18 - 4 =$ but became very distressed when set the problem: 'There are 4 fewer boys than girls in the class. There are 18 girls in the class. How many boys are in the class?'

What does the practitioner need to do?

- Create opportunities for children to use number language.
- Link the child's fascination for counting to real items.
- Build on any particular strengths in mathematical skills. Help the child show someone else what to do.
- As mathematical problems are introduced, make them realistic and close to the child's own experience.
- Continue to offer concrete number materials as the child is likely to have some difficulty with abstract number concepts.

4. Knowledge and understanding of the world

To give young children with autism the best opportunities for developing their knowledge and understanding of the world, practitioners will need to pay particular attention to:

- offering activities which give a range of opportunities for firsthand experience;
- helping the child reflect on those experiences and recognise his role in them;
- helping the child to draw upon past experiences to help him anticipate, predict, problem solve and make choices.

Learning	Teaching
Within this area of learning, children develop the knowledge, skills and understanding to help them make sense of the world.	The practitioner has an important role in triggering curiosity in the young child with autism – who may not be naturally inquisitive.
The young child with autism may be confused rather than curious about his surroundings.	The Early Years practitioner will need to act as an interpreter for the young child with autism – helping him to make sense of past, present and future events.

Stepping Stones	*Examples of what children do*
Some young children with autism show extreme curiosity for certain things.	Every day when the nursery children played out, David went round the garden area lifting stones to see what insects and worms he could see. He made no attempt to show others his discoveries.
The child may have a fascination for technology.	If the computer was switched on, Henry monopolised it.
Most young children with autism are quick to notice even the smallest changes in layout or routine.	Lucy was distressed on arrival at the crèche. It turned out that her favourite chair had been moved to the other side of the room.
Young children with autism are slow to develop an awareness of self.	Jack would check his facial expression in a mirror to see what he was feeling.

What does the practitioner need to do?

- Start from the child's own interests, no matter how unusual. Encourage him to share these with others. Help him record the interest through drawing, writing, making a model, taking a photograph.
- Note what sort of changes are likely to cause distress and either avoid them or give the child clear warning, supported by visual clues.
- Set up simple problem-solving tasks, e.g. trying to work out how to operate a particular action toy.
- Help the child draw on past experience to answer the question, 'What will happen if . . .?'
- Use an interest in computers as an opportunity to increase the child's ICT skills.
- Help the child develop an idea of the sequence of time from past to present, perhaps using photographs.
- Encourage the child to ask questions.
- Introduce language to describe emotions.
- Link this language of emotion to actual events and actions.
- Use opportunities to explain the emotions others must be feeling, drawing the child's attention to body language and facial expression.

5. Physical development
To give young children with autism the best opportunities for physical development, practitioners will need to pay particular attention to:

- helping the child recognise what is safe and unsafe in physical activity;
- overcoming any anxiety the child has related to physical activity;
- helping the child relate positively to other children during physical activities.

Learning	Teaching
Within this area of learning, children develop skills of co-ordination and movement.	Practitioners will need to be vigilant with those young children with autism whose agility outstrips their sense of danger.
Stepping stones At first, the young child with autism may find going into another room for PE very challenging. Asked to 'find a partner', the young child with autism is likely to seem bewildered.	*Examples of what children do* Danny would go into the hall, but tried to stay near the walls. He seemed fearful of crossing the big space. All the other children rushed to get into twos. Bradley saw another child approach him and turned away.

What does the practitioner need to do?

- Have clear safety rules which the child can understand.
- Give the child opportunities to explore the space available in his own time – at first perhaps when no other children are present.
- Help the young child with autism understand the language of co-operation as it relates to physical activity – such as 'wait' and 'take turns', using picture cues.
- Model 'finding a partner', and make sure the child understands what each partner has to do.
- Spend some time specifically teaching imitation skills which involve body actions and movement.
- Help the young child with autism initiate games such as 'tig'. (Tim was helped to use a PECS card to start this game. He would hand it to another child who then had to chase him.)
- Help the child recognise when he needs help and how to ask for it.

6. Creative development

To give young children with autism the best opportunities for developing creative skills, practitioners will need to pay particular attention to:

- offering a wide range of activities to which the child can respond by using many senses;
- giving the child sufficient time to explore and begin to develop ideas;
- using the real and concrete as a starting point for activities which become pretend and abstract;
- prompting the child to make connections between past and present experiences.

Learning	Teaching
Within this area of learning, children become aware of different options and choices. They begin to make connections between one area of learning and another, extending their understanding. The area also includes role-play and imaginative play	Early Years practitioners have a key role in supporting children in developing independence and making choices. Practitioners can help the young child with autism reflect on previous experiences and learning – guiding them to make connections between past and present learning.
Stepping stones	*Examples of what children do*
Some young children with autism actively resist messy activities. Variety of experience is rarely sought by the young child with autism. The child is likely to have a very literal understanding of what a particular object is for, and be slow in developing the idea that one object can represent another. The child may put on clothes from the dressing up box, but be unable to take on the role of someone else.	Danielle would paint with a brush, but not with a sponge. Ryan loved the sand tray – when it was available, he wouldn't try any other activities. The nursery teacher had a plastic banana and pretended to eat it. Gemma copied her. Then the teacher held the banana to her ear and spoke into it as if it was a telephone. Gemma looked shocked and shouted 'No'. Children were putting on aprons and pretending to cook. Mitchell put on an apron, but just played with the train set.

What does the practitioner need to do?

- Offer a variety of textures and sensory experiences and discover what the child can tolerate.
- If a child heads for one activity to the exclusion of all other play opportunities, don't have that activity available every day – or just bring it out for part of the session.
- Get involved in play activities and 'push' the child's imagination. Rosie was sitting inside a 'boat' constructed by other children. The teacher put her hand into the 'water' and 'splashed' another child. That child 'splashed' the teacher – who dramatically wiped the 'water' from her face. The teacher then 'splashed' Rosie who laughed and 'splashed' the teacher back.
- Encourage role-play by starting with people and situations very familiar to the child.
- Support children in making choices by limiting the options available.
- Help children recall and review things they have already done – use photographs to help.

Play in pre-school education

The emphasis on a play-based approach to delivering an Early Years curriculum is generally welcomed and recognised by Early Years practitioners. Indeed, the role of play as a medium for Early Years curriculum delivery has been emphasised by the Department for Education and Employment (2000) in the *Curriculum Guidance for the Foundation Stage*.

Neaum and Tallack (1997) in their excellent book, *Good Practice in Implementing the Pre-school Curriculum*, advise the reader that all pre-school curriculum models 'are based on the notion that children learn through active involvement with their environment and that this is best achieved through play'. They examine influential approaches to pre-school education, e.g.

- Rudolph Steiner's approach based on the notion that creative fantasy is a very important aspect of pre-school years and that up to seven years is the age of imitation;
- Maria Montessori – who argued that 'play is a child's work' and built her approach on that principle;
- High Scope – where Piaget's psychological theory of learning underpins the learning through play approach.

Neaum and Tallack recommend that, 'Play, as a medium for curriculum delivery, is recognised as the most appropriate way for young children to learn.' However, it constitutes a difficulty for those involved in educating young children with autism, since difficulties in developing play skills characterise autism in the Early Years.

Play in autism

Children with autism typically do not develop play skills in accord with the usual developmental pattern. Indeed, lack or impairment of imaginative play skills characterises the third area of the triad of impairments. However, emphasis on the noticeable lack of imaginative play development in the pre-school years has perhaps distracted attention from the atypical development of functional play skills which precede symbolic and imaginative play in normal development. Williams *et al.* (1999) point up the tendencies of children with autism to relate to objects in idiosyncratic ways, e.g.

- odd patterns of visual inspection, such as twisting an object close to the eye;
- spending long periods intensely scrutinising just one object, or a single part of an object;
- preferring to use the proximal senses of touch and taste;
- use of sniffing and mouthing to explore odour and texture;
- spending longer periods on simple manipulative play (mouthing, waving, banging) than on more functional and symbolic play – even when mental age rather than chronological age is taken into account;
- stereotypical behaviours such as putting objects in rows, piling objects on top of one another, or repeatedly ordering and reordering objects;
- odd or unusual responses to some objects – either being fascinated or very fearful;
- functional play, when present, is not as frequent or varied as would be expected.

Additionally, children with autism have difficulty in using the joint attention strategies which would help them develop skills with objects, their imitation skills are poorly developed and they rarely look to adults to demonstrate object use.

The implications for play skill development are that children with autism require direct teaching of object function/toy use in structured situations. The practitioner should ensure that early play skills including manipulative and exploratory play and skilful play with a range of materials are developing before embarking on the teaching of functional, symbolic, pretend, fantasy and dramatic play. The developmental progression in the Observation Profile (Chapter 7) may be helpful here.

Functional play is the appropriate use of an object in play, for example pushing a car along the ground, or associating objects in a conventional way – for example, putting a spoon to the mouth of a doll, or a pan on a toy cooker (Ungerer and Sigman 1981, cited in Williams *et al.* 1999). These are not necessarily acts of pretence however as the objects may be treated as small real objects, rather than 'pretend' objects.

Children with autism spend less time playing functionally than others matched for expressive language and general mental age. Such play is less varied and integrated and is characterised by repetitive manipulations such as continuously loading and unloading a truck or repeatedly crashing an aeroplane. Adrian, aged 4, stacked aeroplanes on top of buses and placed pilot and driver figures in each – but his 'play' stopped there and could not be extended.

There is further evidence of specific impairment of spontaneous symbolic pretend play in young children with autism (Harris 1993, Jarrold *et al.* 1996). Young children with autism are less likely to play spontaneously with toys in the appropriate way or to develop simple pretend play. They rarely spontaneously produce more advanced types of pretend play such as using one object as a substitute for another, making a doll act or creating imaginary objects or beings (Baron-Cohen 1987, Lewis and Boucher 1988).

However, children with autism can be prompted to produce examples of pretend play as Lewis and Boucher in their 1988 and 1990 studies demonstrated. They used simple props and figures and asked children to show what could be done with them. For example, handed a toy car and a piece of string, one child placed the string on the car and said 'Get petrol'. But even when children with autism evidence the ability to pretend, they produce fewer novel play acts (Jarrold *et al.* 1996) and their play remains repetitive and inflexible. This provides a challenge in creating intervention programmes since it is possible for the child to produce a detailed sequence of pretend play which at first sight looks delightfully imaginative. Lucy, a young child with autism in a Reception class, was observed with a doll's house and miniature toys. She got the doll out of bed, gave her breakfast, took her to the park – on the swing, slide and roundabout, took her home again and put her to bed. The visiting psychologist was bemused to see this apparent imaginative play sequence. At a follow-up visit a few weeks later Lucy was observed again. Again she got the doll up, gave her breakfast, took her to the park where she went in the same order on the swing, the slide and the roundabout. The 'imaginary play' sequence was, in fact, a learned routine, acquired in the course of her speech and language therapy sessions. Harris (1993) suggests that while children with autism may be prompted into producing genuine make-believe play, they have difficulty spontaneously generating and developing their own pretend creations.

Approaches to developing play

It is, therefore, essential for practitioners to recognise that rather than teaching through play, play itself has to be taught to children with autism.

Interactive play

Given that the propensity to play emerges very early and spontaneously in normal development this presents an unusual challenge. If we teach a set of play routines, the child with autism may acquire these and yet engage in them merely as a set of learned routines. The attitude for play also has to be elicited; that is, a sense of fun, of unpredictability, of creativity and entertainment. A good place to start is early interactive play. 'Intensive interaction' and 'Musical interaction', described in Chapter 4, provide examples of approaches to stimulating early interactive play.

Phil Christie and Wendy Prevezer (1998) outline strategies for developing skills fundamental to intentional communication. Engaging in these, the child is learning to play. They describe:

- imitating
- play routines
- set songs
- flexible songs
- developing give and take.

The first steps consist of 'tuning in' to the child so that eventually he will 'tune in' to you. Ideas for eliciting **imitation** include imitating the child's vocal sounds, matching pitch and volume as well as rhythm and actual sounds; joining in with his walking, jumping, stamping; joining in playing simple instruments and making a dialogue. Commenting either in speech or song on the child's actions can help to set up a 'dialogue' as with Ricky in the example given in Chapter 4. The rhythmic musical commentary engages the child's attention so that pauses and exaggerated 'gaps' are noticed and the child begins to fill them in. Simple sung commentary is effective in helping the child to 'tune in'.

'Peek-a-boo' and other **play routines** such as 'Round and round the garden' and 'I'm coming to get you!', with appropriate use of timing, pausing, anticipation and climax, can prove fun to young children with autism well beyond the age at which they would usually be used. It is not unusual to find that a relatively skilful four-, five- or six-year-old with autism or Asperger syndrome will enjoy an unexpected game of 'peek-a-boo'. Five year old Damien had made a plasticine ring with help from his support assistant. One of the authors held the ring to her eye, saying, 'peek-a-boo'. Damien giggled. An interactive game developed – despite this being the sort of play usually enjoyed during the first year of life, Damien was amused and entertained by it.

Set songs such as 'Wind the bobbin up', 'Row your boat' and 'The wheels on the bus' benefit from repetition. Again, the use of dramatic pauses, allowing the child opportunities to take the lead, changing the pace and volume, allowing the child to choose the pace and volume can create variety in the routine.

Christie and Prevezer also suggest using familiar tunes such as 'Here we go round the Mulberry Bush' to create **flexible songs** by changing the words to suit the situation, e.g. 'This is the way we get in the car'.

In developing **'give and take'**, the aim is to share control of the songs, building elements of teasing and surprise.

Throughout, the emphasis on active involvement, on having fun, on developing variety within routines, on creating an awareness of building to a climax, of teasing, surprise and shared laughter creates an atmosphere of play. Christie and Prevezer are currently preparing a handbook on 'Interactive Play' with detailed ideas.

Developing simple play structures

Beyer and Gammeltoft (2000) argue for a close connection between emotional, social and cognitive developmental aspects of play. They outline play strategies to develop:

- attention, expectation and shared focus;
- imitation and mirroring;
- parallel play and play dialogue;
- script and social stories;
- shifts in taking turns;
- games and rules in playing.

For all play sessions a **'stage is set'** to mark out the area where play activities take place. Simple, recognisable toys which motivate the child are collected into a box. There are two sets so that the adult has exactly the same toys as the child. As in interactive play the adult begins by imitating the child's actions, reinforcing the child's initiatives. The adult is then able to guide play rather than take over.

Exaggeration is a feature in the earliest stages when big and conspicuous toys are used, e.g. spinning tops, telephones, soap guns.

Parallel play is then developed, using a table, divided by coloured tape, as a stage. The adult, with a replica set of miniature toys, again mirrors the child's play sequence and gradually provides new ideas. This phase is replicated with two children playing in parallel. Toys prompt the play, for example a small cake with candles may trigger the dolls having a birthday party.

In **visual scripting**, a picture story accompanied by matching toys prompts the child to play out the story. The judicious use of additional toys introduces some variety.

Social stories, developed by Carol Gray (1997), can be used to prompt play activities using puppets or dolls. Here, the child himself is the main character and this increases motivation.

Taking turns in games is developed using props such as a cap worn to indicate whose turn it is.

Different coloured bands can be used to indicate roles in **group games**, e.g. choosing, leading.

Beyer and Gammeltoft's book contains clear instructions and photographs.

Developing symbolic and pretend play

Sherratt (1999) has taught pretend play within a social group of children with autism and others with learning difficulty. The key steps of the approach included:

- an adult modelling a number of pretend play scenarios in front of a group of children who watched, sitting in a semi-circle;
- the children were encouraged to imitate and extend the play scenarios in pairs or individually, while the others watched;
- videos of the scenarios were subsequently shown to the children and the most important features identified;
- new materials and new scenarios were modelled for the children in later sessions.

Sherratt emphasises the importance of **narrative structure**, a framework which provides the child with a reason to start, a framework of events and an end product. Very familiar scenarios include:

- classic children's stories such as 'Red Riding Hood', 'The Three Little Pigs' and 'Goldilocks and the Three Bears', which offer stereotyped characters, repetitive phrasing and an affective 'hook line', e.g. the mounting threat as Red Riding Hood notices 'What big eyes, ears, teeth' that 'grandma' has;

- current video/film stories familiar to the child; 'Toy Story' would be a good starting point for Joshua who was already sitting on a shelf in his bedroom pretending to be 'Woody';
- the child's own interests, e.g. trains or dinosaurs can be developed into stories to act out.

Also important is **affect**, that is, emotional engagement. Fun and excitement are crucial if this sort of play is to become spontaneous. Slapstick, obvious humour, pantomime and melodrama can be very effective in securing the emotional engagement of the child. The parent, teacher or other Early Years practitioner has to play too! And enjoy it!

As Sherratt notes, '**non-representational play materials** are a core feature of symbolic pretend play'. Boxes, pieces of cloth, ribbons, string, plasticine, large wooden blocks, balloons and sticks can be used in many different ways, while the use of representational props – puppets and dolls – helps to maintain the structure of the play.

There is a need to **make the pretence explicit**. Symbolic demands have to be built up in a structured way, and the act of pretence labelled, as children with autism may not easily distinguish 'pretence' from 'reality' very clearly (as we will see with Gemma and her 'baby whales', see p. 74), or may not switch from one to the other very readily.

The adult setting up the play situation will need to **use appropriate language levels**. Simple language, communicating an affective as well as semantic meaning should be used rather than complex structures, e.g. 'Ow! Hot chimney. Burnt'.

Further ideas for developing pretend play may be found in Dave Sherratt's article, and the reader is recommended to see him in action (dressed in a sheet, turning into a jellyfish!) to be enthused as to the possibilities.

Developing social play

Wolfberg (1999) noted that children with autism are capable of engaging in more complex and diverse forms of play when supported by an adult, and also when supported by more capable peers. This led her to design interventions for children with autism involving participation in play in integrated settings together with more competent peers. Basically, the model builds on the work of Vygotsky (1966, 1978) who emphasised the critical role of play as a cultural/social activity, providing for the acquisition of:

- symbolic capacities
- interpersonal skills
- social knowledge.

The components of the integrated play approach are:

- **Novice and expert players** – three to five children with a higher ratio of typically developing peers and/or siblings to children with special needs.
- **Playgroup guide** – these may be teachers, therapists, psychologists, parents and other care providers.
- **Settings** – where children would naturally play: home, playgroup, nursery, class group, recreation centre.
- **Schedule and routines** – regular meetings lasting 30 minutes to one hour are held once or twice a week for an extended period. Visual timetables (see TEACCH) help children anticipate sessions. Opening and closing routines are established, e.g. plan, review, clean-up, finishing song, together with rules for behaviour.
- **Play environment** – clearly defined boundaries are established and play materials clearly organised and labelled.
- **Assessing play** – play is systematically observed, distinguishing non-differentiated object manipulation, functional, and symbolic/pretend play. Distinctions are also

made on the social dimension, between isolation, orientation/onlooker, proximity/parallel, common focus and common goal. The ways in which children communicate in peer play are also scrutinised, i.e. functions of communication such as requests for objects, peer interaction, protests, declarations and comments. Children's play preferences are also noted – toys and props, play activities, play themes, playmates. The Observation Profile (Chapter 7) provides for that area of assessment.

- **Enhancing play** – the intervention, guided participation, involves structuring opportunities for the novice player to co-ordinate play and also to practise newer, more complex play forms.
- **Monitoring play initiations** – observations are made of all the initiations children make in play, however unusual, and indicate present and emerging capacities in play.
- **Scaffolding interactions** – scaffolding consists of the provision of adjustable and temporary support structures. The adult acts as interpreter to help the novice players and the 'experts' understand each other's actions and words. The adult may:
  – direct the play event and model behaviour by identifying common themes, arranging props, assigning roles and play partners;
  – guide the children by posing leading questions, commenting on activities, offering suggestions and giving subtle reminders using verbal and visual cues;
  – gradually reduce support and move to the periphery.
- **Social communication guidance** strategies foster attempts to extend play invitations to peers, respond to peers' cues and initiations in play, maintain and expand interactions with peers and join peers in an established play event.
- **Play guidance** allows children to be fully immersed in play and engaged in activities slightly beyond their capacity. Wolfberg gives an example of a child who lines up objects, incorporating this into a larger play theme of pretending to shop for groceries. With the help of more capable peers, the child may be encouraged to be the assistant arranging groceries on the shelf. Children are thus encouraged to go beyond their present ability to explore and diversify routines.

Summary

- Play in young children with autism is relatively impoverished, impaired or absent.
- Children with autism have to learn **to** play, rather than being taught *through* play.
- Children with autism may develop the capacity for play at later ages and stages than typically developing peers. It is important not to miss the opportunity.
- Play development can be encouraged, following a developmental pattern broadly similar to that usually occurring spontaneously, i.e.
  – early interactive play
  – functional play
  – symbolic and pretend play
  – social play.
- Fun, humour, enjoyment and excitement characterise play which needs to happen at the level at which the child is comfortable – use of the Observation Profile (Chapter 7), may be helpful here.
- The adult involved in eliciting, encouraging and developing play has to be involved in playing too.
- Social integration in playgroups can be used to prompt, produce and extend play routines – it is important to involve more able peers in the groups.

6 Behavioural difficulties – from understanding to intervention

Difficulties in coping with their child's behaviour are frequently reported by the parents of young children with autism. Early Years staff in nursery school, nursery class or playgroup experience similar problems.

Richard, blue eyed and blond, looked angelic sitting in his pushchair as his mother pushed him round the estate. Equally so in church on Sunday until his high pitched screams disrupted the sermon and then the prayers. His mother tried to keep him outdoors for as long as possible.

Ellis, aged three, caused tremendous disruption in his nursery class by his apparent refusal to follow instructions, his ability to 'switch off' to all attempts at interaction and his stubborn determination to play with the train set all morning.

Sam, aged two, caused similar disruption at the College crèche. His young mother was asked to remove him, as was Lee's mother, a nurse who had placed her highly active two and a half year old in the hospital nursery.

Mark's parents had been successful in finding a private nursery school for their three year old, but despaired of 'getting through to him'. The only way of preventing his enraged temper tantrums at home or in the nursery seemed to be to allow him to run up and down on tiptoes, occasionally stopping to spin, or to let him sit in a corner repetitively flicking the pages of his favourite books.

Assessment and diagnosis will lead to a developing understanding of the nature of autism and access to appropriate educational support. However, difficulties in coping with the young child's behaviour often continue to worry parents and Early Years practitioners.

If we consider the nature of the core impairments in autism we can clearly see how and why such behavioural difficulties occur (see Figure 6.1.).

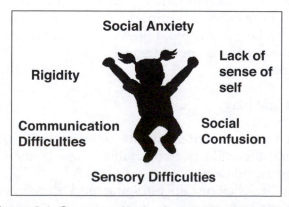

Figure 6.1 Sources of behavioural difficulties in autism

Sources of behavioural difficulties in young children with autism

Social impairment

Alison Gopnik's (1993) imaginative portrayal of how young children with autism might experience other human beings (see Chapter 3, p. 31) vividly conveys the difficulties they will experience in interpreting other people's behaviour and in forming any sort of ability to predict their likely actions. When one of the authors momentarily left her 18 month old daughter in the living room with strict instructions 'Not to touch the CD player', she returned to find her crouched on the unit, face crumpled in a look of shamed guilt, anticipating Mum's likely reaction. The 18 month old with autism is not able to anticipate in this way and social constraints do not operate to control (or almost control!) behaviour.

Lacking the ability to interpret and predict others' behaviour, the young child with autism also lacks strategies for affecting others' behaviour and will attempt to meet his needs head-on – walking through and over obstacles, even if these happen to be other children. He may grab or snatch at what he wants, often expressing rage when his needs are not met immediately. Or even, without anger, simply not understanding a basic social approach. When the nursery nurse stretched out her hand to lead Rebecca away from the sand tray – Rebecca bit it!

Difficulties with communication

Difficulties in understanding how to communicate or even being aware that communication is possible lead to frustration, anger and anxiety in young children with autism. Emily, listening to a music tape in the playroom, began to scream and cry when the tape finished, unaware of the possibility of running to her mother in the next room to get her help.

Even when spoken language is being acquired it's not always used to communicate effectively. When faced with a puzzling task or situation, three year old Adam cries, 'I can't believe it's not butter!'

Lack of self-awareness

The child's lack of awareness of his own intentions has been identified as characteristic of autism by Powell and Jordan (1993). Thus the child's behaviour is triggered by external stimuli and is not under his own conscious control. At an even more basic level, lack of bodily awareness and an absent or very limited sense of control may be involved in the difficulties experienced. An example is toileting where some children become very afraid of the toilet, or in eating where children may restrict themselves to one or two known tastes, smells, colours or textures.

And in terms of more advanced skills, as Powell and Jordan point out, if the child has poor self-awareness he is likely to lack awareness of any alternative strategies for coping and will stick rigidly to one learned response.

Sensory difficulties

Unusual sensory responses in autism are well documented. Grandin and Scariano (1986) and Williams (1998) describe vividly their experiences of sensory and perceptual difficulties in autism. 'For me', Williams writes, 'sensory hypersensitivity is a fluctuating condition' and 'hypersensitive touch, hearing or vision are examples of sensory over-firing'. Very often the young child with autism's aversion to social situations may originate in sensory hypersensitivity to, for example, the visit to the playgroup, the dining hall, the supermarket.

73

On the other hand, lack of sensory response can cause difficulties. Ciara touched the gas fire when her mother was in the kitchen, burning her hand badly. Her mother only discovered what had happened when she came back into the living room and saw the wound. Ciara hadn't cried. Adrian has no awareness of the danger of the cooker and will grab at the pans of hot food if he can get to them. When his mother took the casserole from the oven using oven gloves, Adrian went to lift it himself without the gloves. He cried only when his mother took hold of his hands to run them under the cold tap.

Sensory responses may be entirely idiosyncratic. Tom, who liked to sniff things, repeatedly attacked a certain teacher in his special school. By a process of elimination, the staff identified a particular perfume as the trigger. Only on the days when she wore this fragrance was she attacked!

Rigidity

The 'insistence on sameness' found in autism frequently leads to the experience of behavioural difficulties. Simon only drank milk from a full bottle. If the bottle was a centimetre short of full when offered to him, a major tantrum would ensue. Bobby liked to line up his toy animals, one of which had a half-turned head. His failed attempts to get this one to face the same way as the others drove him into fits of rage. Alex made a complicated structure which he called his 'couch motor'. This sat on the living room settee. Any attempt to move it provoked a passionate outburst. Repetitive and stereotypic behaviours may develop, including hand-flapping, rocking, spinning or unusual obsessions. Frith (1989) has speculated that in an incomprehensible world such rituals may serve as a white stick to the blind. Alternatively, some repetitive or ritualised behaviour may be rewarding as a form of self-stimulation.

Impaired or delayed imaginative development may cause difficulty. Gemma, aged five, made her grandmother buy a number of unusually shaped shampoo bottles, then empty them out. She then piled them into her pushchair and used them as 'baby whales'. In the playground, playing at whales, she bit another child. When questioned by her teacher, she said in explanation, 'It was the killer whale'. In Gemma's case there was a lack of ability to appropriately separate the 'imaginary' from the 'real' experience (see Figure 6.2.).

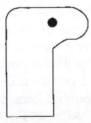

Figure 6.2 Gemma's 'baby whale'

Lack of play and self-help skills

The lack of, or narrow range of play and self-help skills is often a significant factor in the experience of behavioural difficulties in young children with autism. Children with autism lack the means of self-occupation which typically developing children spontaneously acquire through their interest in novelty, their disposition to imitate, their curiosity and social participation. They may then withdraw into a narrow range of familiar behaviours, shutting out still further the social world.

Perspectives on behaviour

Schopler and Mesibov (1995) point out that the experience of autism is different from the points of view of different professionals. For the clinician, the diagnostic criteria may define autism and appropriately so. For the teacher and parent, however, difficulties in learning and behaviour are more prominent and for each, different difficulties predominate.

Teachers' perspectives

Difficulties commonly reported by teachers (Helps *et al.* 1999) include:

Teachers' perspective
• Repetitive/obsessional or bizarre behaviour
• Poor communication
• Aggressive behaviours
• Peer difficulties
• Encouraging self-directed activity
• Resistance to change
• Poor attention and concentration
• Unpredictability of behaviour

Autism perspective

Social Anxiety

Rigidity

Lack of sense of self

Communication Difficulties

Social Confusion

Sensory Difficulties

Figure 6.3 Teachers' perspectives on behaviour

In order to intervene effectively it will be necessary for us as educators to go beyond an immediate response to the surface behaviour and to attempt to understand the function or the purpose of the behaviour from the point of view of the child. In our previous book, Cumine *et al.* 1998, we used the analogy of the lens of interpretation to look at the behaviour and the events in context. This would equally apply in our attempts to understand and respond to apparent behavioural difficulties in the young child with autism, see Figure 6.4.

The teacher, parent, therapist or other involved practitioner, may need to try more than one 'lens of interpretation' and will in best practice consult with others when attempting to intervene and bring about changes in behaviour. Reference to Chapters 3 and 4 should be helpful here.

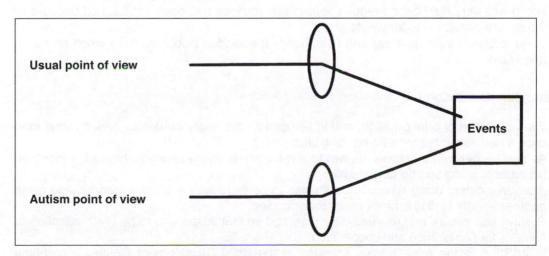

Usual point of view

Events

Autism point of view

Figure 6.4 The autism lens of interpretation

Case study example (1) Justin (aged three years)

> **Behaviour Concerns:**
> Temper outbursts
> Head-banging
> Limited diet
> Poor sleep pattern

Three year old Justin, one of triplets, caused his parents concern from the age of 15 months, when his main problems were outbursts of temper during which he would often bang his head. Triggers were difficult to identify but seemed to range from falling over and stubbing his toe to being given an extra piece of toast. Parents described Justin as a 'control freak'. For example, offered a video to watch, he flung it across the room. He then became increasingly angry as alternative videos were offered. Eventually, an enraged Justin marched across the room, retrieved the original video and inserted it himself.

Justin began to bang his head with such severity that on one occasion he ended up in A&E with two black eyes and a damaged nose. Justin would bang his head on the floor, wall or door. If his mother walked away, he would run after her and recommence banging his head in front of her.

At two and a half years of age, when diagnosed with an autistic spectrum disorder, Justin would only eat crisps and drink juice. He would wake at 5.30 or 6.00 a.m. and start to scream or head-bang until all the family were awake.

Original intervention

- Justin's concerned mother read about 'time out' procedures in a magazine. She began to respond to his anger and head-banging by taking him to his bedroom.
- Once there, Justin would bang his head violently on the bedroom door and call out 'hold hands' to indicate that he wanted to come down.
- When his mother went to get him, he refused and began screaming and banging his head again. This would happen several times until Justin finally came downstairs.
- Father, if at home during these incidents, would go and sit in Justin's bedroom, anxious about his safety. Justin was always cuddled when he came down from his bedroom.

The **autism lens** showed that:

- Justin was extremely stressed – as were his parents.
- Justin's head-banging and temper outbursts produced the effect of removing any unpleasant experience or gaining a desired end.
- Although Justin had some language, he was unable to communicate his needs effectively.
- Justin had few play and self-help skills other than watching videos or looking at books.
- Justin was very rigid but no regular behavioural routines had been established because of the severe disruption to family life.
- Justin suffered from glue ear and head-banging episodes would intensify when he had a head cold.

Planned intervention I

- Time out to be of brief duration, and to be used as the angry behaviour began rather than once it had escalated to head-banging pitch.
- As Justin's behaviour calmed, he was to come down from the bedroom himself, rather than his parents going up and down to him.
- After an incident using time out, Justin was to be dealt with in a calm manner, and given another activity to distract him, rather than cuddled.
- Positive behaviours and rewards were identified so that Justin was to be given attention or rewards for compliance and cooperation.
- In addition to the once weekly sessions at the Child Development Centre, a part-time placement in a specialist nursery class was obtained where Justin began to acquire learning and play skills.

Planned intervention II

- Justin was subsequently given a full-time placement with a special support assistant as part of an experimental scheme to offer early intensive intervention to young children with autistic spectrum disorders. Specialist teacher support was also provided.
- The teacher and special support assistant also worked with Justin's mother for two hours a week.
- Justin's communication, learning and social skills improved rapidly and within one year, placement in a mainstream reception class with support was possible.
- Justin's mother reported that his behaviour was now 'better' than that of the other triplets.

Case study example (2) Bashar (aged three years)

> **Behaviour Concerns:**
> Destruction of nursery equipment
> Hurting others
> Limited diet
> Poor sleep pattern

Three year old Bashar entered the open area in his nursery 'like a whirlwind'. One sweep of his arm cleared the plants from the window ledge. While everyone ran to rescue the plants, the sand would be tipped into the water, which was, in turn, showered round the room. Any child encountered would be bowled over. Any adult who did not move out of the way quickly was liable to be bitten or kicked.

Bashar had no language, was highly impulsive and showed no awareness of the needs of the others in his world. His main source of food was milk – which he insisted on having from a bottle. No regular sleep pattern had been established. His parents were exhausted. Mother would easily burst into tears and father didn't know which way to turn.

Original intervention

- Bashar was initially seen as a 'naughty boy'. He was chastised and expected to calm down.
- He was assigned a special support assistant, but hurt her repeatedly as she tried to constrain his behaviour.

The **autism lens** showed that:

- Bashar was overwhelmed by the bright and colourful displays at nursery.
- He couldn't cope with having to make choices.
- He was unable to cope with the sheer numbers of other children and the corresponding noise levels.
- He was unable to understand much of what was said to him.

Planned intervention

- An activity which Bashfar found rewarding was identified – he enjoyed being spun in a large 'dish' in the playground.
- A photograph of the 'dish' was taken and included in Bashar's visual timetable (see TEACCH in Chapter 4).
- This activity was used as a way of making contact with Bashar, as he was encouraged to give eye contact before being spun (see 'Intensive interaction', pp. 42–44).
- Other interactive activities helped to develop Bashar's communication skills.
- Bashar was given opportunities to have some time away from the big open space in nursery in quieter, less stressful areas.
- Bashar was offered activities designed to relax him, e.g. foot massage.
- His play skills were developed using one toy at a time – so as not to overwhelm him.

- He was given the opportunity to try an activity in the quiet area before going to a similar activity in the main area.
- Staff simplified the language they used when speaking to Bashar.
- Desired behaviours were reinforced immediately.

Bashar managed to access the main nursery room for short periods and engage in the rehearsed activities. He began to engage in meaningful eye contact, and finger pointing started to develop. Subsequently Bashar joined the Reception class at a school for children with severe learning difficulties, where strategies to develop his communication, social and play skills continued.

Case study example (3) Joshua (aged five years)

> **Behaviour Concerns:**
>
> Following 'own agenda'
>
> Reluctance to participate in group activities
>
> Screaming and wailing

Five year old Joshua was in the Reception/Year 1 class at a school for children with moderate learning difficulties. He had previously attended a mainstream nursery class and Reception class with additional support.

When the teacher attempted to include Joshua in activities he would wander off, sometimes trying to leave the classroom – and the school building. He had learned to stand on a chair in order to reach the classroom door handle. He was also obsessed with the classroom windows – closing them if they were open, but opening them if they were closed. He would climb up shelving in order to reach the window handles.

Joshua was also fascinated by light switches, plug sockets, computer and video wiring, fire extinguishers and radiator valves. For health and safety reasons, his teacher could not 'tactically' ignore these behaviours.

Joshua would scream and wail for no apparent reason.

Original intervention

- Joshua was assigned a special support assistant.
- If he screamed and wailed or tried to climb up to the windows, she used a favourite toy to distract him or took him for a walk round the school – something he enjoyed.
- When the other children went into the school hall (something he particularly disliked) Joshua remained in the classroom with the support assistant.
- A whole-class picture timetable was introduced – but only used at the beginning of the day.

 The **autism lens** showed that:

- Joshua found it hard to cope with the proximity of his peers.
- He wasn't able to work out what was expected of him – particularly when one activity ended and another began.
- He was further confused by different sets of expectations – one set when all the children were in the classroom, another set when he was alone in the room with his support assistant.
- Being taken for a walk or given a favourite activity was having the effect of reinforcing the screaming/wailing/climbing, by acting as a reward etc.

Planned intervention

- The whole-class timetable continued to be used – but began to be referred to at transition times throughout the day.
- Joshua had an individual picture timetable, which was used systematically. It included a 'go

for a walk' picture so that desired rather than difficult behaviour could be reinforced. Pictures relating to his favourite activities were also included.

- A work station was set up in a quiet area of the classroom, together with a basket system to help Joshua focus on each task (see TEACCH, Chapter 4).
- Staff began to be more consistent with rules and expectations.
- Joshua was to be removed from potentially dangerous situations in a low-key way, but staff began to exaggerate their praise for desired behaviour.
- Joshua began to be brought to group activities once the other children had settled, as he seemed to find this less threatening.
- There was a gradual introduction of one child at a time to activities Joshua had chosen.

Joshua's screaming and wailing have now almost been eliminated, and he is generally much calmer.

The time he is prepared to sit beside peers has increased, and he has begun to make a contribution to group activities.

His access to the curriculum has extended. Skills he has developed with support at his work station are increasingly generalised in the wider classroom setting.

Parents' perspectives

Difficulties commonly experienced by parents (van Bourgondien 1993) include:

Parents' perspective	Autism perspective
- Aggression - Eating problems - Non-compliance - Sleep problems - Toileting problems - Lack of initiative - Lack of response to discipline - Poor play skills	Social Anxiety Rigidity Lack of sense of self Communication Difficulties Social Confusion

Figure 6.5 Parents' perspectives

Normally developing children in the preschool years are reported to present a number of common problems, including toilet training, fears, sleeping, bad habits, non-compliance and aggression (Schroede *et al.* 1983, cited by van Bourgondien 1993). van Bourgondien points out that preschool years are reported to present the most difficult time for parents of children with autism (de Myer 1979, in van Bourgondien 1993).

Again, if we turn our autism lens of interpretation on the behaviours and the underlying difficulties, a range of intervention strategies based on an understanding of autism can be suggested.

Aggression and temper tantrums

In the course of normal development physical aggression, related often to difficulties in sharing or frustrated desires, tends to decrease as children acquire the ability to communicate more efficiently and to generate alternative solutions to their problems.

In children with autism, aggression is often related to:

- their impaired or absent communicative ability;
- their rigidity or compulsion to adhere to a set routine or route;
- unusual sensory experience;

- lack of awareness of their own or others' feelings;
- lack of ability to foresee the consequences of their actions;
- impaired ability to generate alternative solutions.

Alan's behaviour at the Child Development Centre provides an example:

- Teacher places a packet of chocolate buttons just out of his reach, and draws Alan's attention to them, hoping to prompt a communicative gesture or point.
- Instead, Alan screams in rage and frustration, throwing himself on the floor, kicking his shoes off, flailing about with his arms and legs to anyone who approaches him.

The **autism lens** would show us that Alan's underlying difficulties were:

- He does not have the means of communicating his strong wish to have the sweets.
- At home he climbs with great agility to reach anything he wants, but in this case there is nothing to climb on.
- At home his temper rules his mother who loves him dearly and hates to see him distressed. Her only strategy is to let him have what he wants immediately.
- Alan is very rigid in his behaviour patterns.
- Alan is of very limited cognitive ability.
- Unbeknown to the Centre's staff, Alan has been awake all night. He is very tired and his ability to tolerate frustration is reduced.

Strategies for reducing aggression and temper tantrums include:

- Structuring the environment to provide greater understanding through the use of predictable routines and visual cues.
- Providing objects for reference or other visual cues to allow the child to know what is going to happen, e.g. finishing one activity and going on to another.
- Checking out the child's physical and emotional state before presenting challenging learning activities.
- Making a precise analysis of the child's level of functional communication and providing a structured approach to teaching communication skills such as pointing.
- Carefully observing and recording the triggers for, and consequences of, aggressive acts. Where possible, removing those consequences that act as reinforcers, and those acts which serve as triggers.
- Building in calming and relaxing periods throughout the child's day, e.g. using soothing music, soft lighting.

Non-compliance

This is the second most frequent concern reported by parents attending the TEACCH programmes (van Bourgondien 1993). As she points out, the preschool years from two to four years are marked by lack of response or opposition to parental requests in normally developing children, as the process of socialisation takes place. In children with autism, the core difficulty in being able to interact socially with others, compounded by difficulties in language and communication, makes clashes of will almost inevitable. In addition, it is during this period that rigid patterns of behaviour and obsessions begin to dominate.

Again, the most important strategies include:

- using very clear, visual and tangible clues to ensure the child understands requests, e.g. holding up a cup when asking if he wants a drink;
- timing requests and instructions for optimum cooperation;

- giving early warning of the next activity / routine, accompanied by visual / tangible cues, e.g. First food [plate] then Park [bike];

1  2

- reducing demands to avoid conflict, e.g. avoiding long waits / noisy, crowded places;
- using consistent rewards as preferred activities to reinforce compliance in selected simple routinised situations, e.g. coming to sit at the table – attractive toy on the table – instruction to sit, 'Tom, sit', followed by prompt reward, e.g. sip of juice and verbal praise, 'good sitting';
- parallel social interaction programme, e.g. using 'music aided communication' / 'gentle interaction' (see Chapter 4) to enhance social responses;
- provision of functional communication programmes, e.g. PECS (Chapter 4).

Eating problems

Many young children have food fads that restrict their diet. Some young children with autism take this to an extreme; not only do they have a craving for certain foods but it can be that the way that the food is arranged on the plate takes on an overwhelming significance.

A related problem can be that the child doesn't sit at the table to eat; instead he grazes from everyone else's plate or helps himself to food throughout the day and night.

Zane had some unusual cravings: he would seek out washing powder and eat it. Chris would only eat white foods, e.g. mashed potato and ice cream, while Hannah, aged four, still refused to eat lumpy food.

The underlying reasons for eating difficulties include:

- a concentration on detail;
- perseveration, due to rigid thought patterns;
- impulsivity, lack of self-control;
- fear of the new or unknown;
- sensory impairment;
- lack of tolerance of certain foods which can, paradoxically, express itself in increasing the desire for that food group;
- lack of social compliance.

Strategies that have been found useful include:

- don't get hung up on a child's eating patterns, as your tension transfers to the child;
- don't discuss the problem in front of the child;
- try to limit access to foods other than at the times you want the child to eat – grazing all day on biscuits etc. limits access to food at designated meal times – if necessary try a fridge / cupboard lock;
- be aware that certain foods may make the child more hyperactive;
- ignore where possible when the child is eating odd things, as negative attention is a reward;

- when it is impossible to ignore, substitute a pleasurable option or give an immediate negative;
- change only one aspect at a time when introducing new foods, i.e. only the taste or colour or texture to limit the overwhelming of all the senses;
- reduce the food to a combination of a tiny amount of the new in with a large amount of the old and chop it up finely or even liquidise to limit the child's ability to pick it out – add more new as it is accepted;
- use favourite food as a reward for trying the new;
- visual prompts for sitting until everything on the plate is eaten;
- view as a stress factor.

Sleeping

Poor sleeping habits affect the whole family's ability to cope. While some children with autism seem able to cope with the odd hour of snatched sleep the effects of sleep deprivation on the rest of the family is stressful and exhausting. All young babies can take differing lengths of time to develop accepted sleep patterns that tie in with the rest of the family. Some children with autism do not appear to reach this stage. Research has indicated that in the early years in particular, sleep problems are a significant factor in causing parental stress.

The underlying reasons relating to sleep difficulties include:

- hyperactivity;
- impulsivity;
- lack of understanding of what is expected;
- short sleep patterns;
- becomes rigid in routine;
- hypersensitive to external stimulation, e.g. sound, light;
- fear of being alone in the dark;
- lack of exercise.

Michael screamed from the moment of birth and he would only doze for brief periods throughout the day and night. When awake he was hyperactive but could not be occupied with activities that stretched him or tired him out. He spent much of his time engaging in stereotypical behaviours or screaming.

Strategies that have been found helpful include:

- establish a de-stressing bedtime routine involving quiet favoured activities to indicate bedtime;
- have a number of quiet favoured activities available in the bedroom which the child can access to fill in periods of wakefulness;
- reduce outside stimulus by use of curtain linings/blinds, soft music playing in the room;
- avoid initiating a ritual that may become a routine, e.g. bringing the child into your bed – return to the child's room and go through the bedtime routine;
- make the bedroom as secure as possible without putting safety at risk, e.g. install child gates;
- use visual reminders of the time the child can get up and rouse the family;
- consult with health visitor/doctor to confirm that there are no medical problems and that the diet is not increasing hyperactivity;
- sleep medication should only be considered after all other methods have failed.

Toileting problems

Toileting problems can lead to embarrassment and health difficulties. Babies are expected to wear nappies and toddlers to begin to become self-sufficient in their toileting by being able to use the toilet and later clean themselves and wash their hands. Once a young child approaches school age if he is not proficient in his toileting then it can become an issue. As well as the self-help aspect of toileting the questions related to health of constant diarrhoea or constipation and/or urinary infections are an issue.

Ruth has always had problems with constipation. She becomes irritable and non-compliant as her discomfort increases. The only release comes from an enema, and sometimes she needs to go to hospital for assistance. She is becoming more distressed as Mum approaches her with the enemas, which causes more distress. Jamie holds himself all day at school and when he gets home he releases his bowels on the carpet in the living room.

The underlying reasons relating to toileting problems include:

- food tolerance;
- opioid excess;
- lack of social awareness;
- fear of bodily functions;
- fear of toilet;
- poor decision-making skills;
- comfort of nappies hides the feeling of being wet;
- lack of control;
- unaware of own bodily feelings;
- developmental delay;
- poor motor control.

Strategies that have been found useful include:

- take nappy off for periods of time so child can connect feeling wet with urinating;
- teach the connection between passing urine and the toilet/potty, e.g. produce the potty to catch the urine rather than sitting on the potty to wait for the urine;
- use an older child to model what to do on the toilet;
- once the child understands reward all attempts;
- deal with 'accidents' in a very low key manner so they are not rewarded by lots of attention;
- give a young boy something to aim at in the toilet, e.g. table tennis ball;
- check that the child's diet is not exacerbating difficulties – see Opioid Excess theory, pp. 53/4;
- if the child is only comfortable to go in a nappy sit the child on the toilet with the nappy on and stage by stage open the nappy and eventually remove it;
- sit the young child facing the back of the toilet so that the progression to standing is more straightforward.

Keys to prevention

Some general principles for preventing and reducing the occurrence of behavioural difficulties can be identified on the basis of experience, research and practice. Faced with a child experiencing behavioural difficulties, practitioners and parents will be helped by taking a systematic approach.

☐ Understanding the source of the difficulty

This may lead to the immediate elimination of the 'trigger' for the behaviour and in consequence the behaviour itself – as with Tom, when looked at through the lens of sensory experience a solution to the problem became apparent.

☐ Structuring the environment for prevention

In principle, the TEACCH approach (see Chapter 4) acts to eliminate sources of confusion for the child and to give him the means of controlling his environment – see Figure 6.6. Clear boundaries mark out areas for particular activity; objects, pictures or diagrams serve to cue the appropriate behaviour and the classroom may be colour-coded to help the child. One youngster, for example, may have a purple dinner mat, purple coat hook, purple transition board and purple basket.

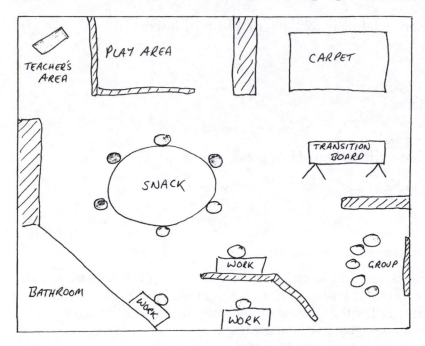

Figure 6.6 A TEACCH Nursery classroom layout

For Matthew, the provision of a TEACCH corner in his Reception class was the key to the start of success in his educational placement following a very fraught nursery year. Here, with a table against the wall, a bookcase alongside, a picture schedule, Smartie reinforcers and coloured counters as tokens, Matthew began to settle and with the security of this base was able to progressively join his peers in various activities.

☐ Providing a means of communication

Given the difficulties in understanding the process of communication and lack of skills in this area, providing a means of communication is a major key to reducing behavioural difficulties in young children with autism. In this respect the introduction of the Picture Exchange Communication System (PECS) has proved a major resource for parents and practitioners. Young children with autism, often without any spoken language, quite quickly learn to offer a picture of the (highly desired) item to obtain it – Emily, described in Chapter 3, exemplifies this.

○━━ Tailoring social demands to the level of the child's ability to cope

Simon, aged four, was screaming in assembly. The social demands were too great so he was allowed first to stay outside the hall with his support assistant, playing with a favourite toy. Gradually, moving closer to the hall, he was introduced first to the doorway, then to the hall itself, accompanied by his support assistant and with a favourite book instead of a toy.

For the young child with autism, the requirements of the Personal, Social and Emotional curriculum will need to be significantly differentiated. Equally, parents of young children with autism quickly learn to avoid demanding social situations such as birthday parties and crowded shops. However, there can be a progression towards being able to cope with these situations.

○━━ Differentiating tasks to the child's level of ability

In terms of learning skills, children with autism have areas of relative strength as well as areas of difficulty. Often there is a 'patchy' profile of abilities. An individual learning plan is therefore essential. The young child with autism may, for example, readily recognise numbers and acquire a sight vocabulary but lack the social skills of interaction and communication which will ultimately make these skills useful.

○━━ Teaching play skills

Again, these do not occur spontaneously. For the young child with autism, early social interaction skills may be developed using rough and tumble play, play routines, lap-games, rhymes and songs. These techniques are included in such approaches as 'Musical interaction' and 'Intensive interaction' (outlined in Chapter 4). Subtler skills of communication may also be developed in such sessions which can be complementary to the skills of communication acquired using PECS. Suggestions for developing play skills are included in Chapter 5.

○━━ Building in positives

In order to promote behavioural change, there is a need to examine the child's experience from the point of view of how positive or how rewarding it is for him. What may appear to us to be a reward, or an interesting experience, may not be so for the child. One inflexible class teacher insisted that Nathan should receive stickers as rewards, 'because all the rest of the children do' – despite the fact that they were meaningless for him. In fact research indicates that the use of 'obsessions' as rewards can be very powerful. Charlop-Christy and Haymes (1998) offered token reinforcers which were objects of obsession in a controlled experiment and found that when working for their particular token/object of obsession, e.g. micro-machine cars/plastic beads/names of video characters, children quickly made progress in their learning tasks. The improvements were marked.

○━━ Allowing for interests/obsessions

It is important to remember that the child's particular preoccupation or 'obsession' is rewarding for him, and in attempting to promote behavioural change they may be effective as outlined above as *rewards* or *reinforcers*.

They may also, as Howlin and Rutter (1987) noted, be useful:

- as an inroad to more acceptable behaviours;
- to facilitate social interaction.

◻─■ Using clear rules

The often rigid disposition of the young child with autism can be turned to advantage in the use of clear and simple rules to govern behaviour. These may also be presented in pictorial sequence to encourage appropriate behaviour. For example: bath/toilet/teeth/bed, see Figure 6.7.

Figure 6.7 A visual timetable in the bathroom

◻─■ De-stressing

Because of the state of confusion or bewilderment in which the young child with autism may often live, high levels of stress may ensue. Similarly the need to intervene in the child's way of controlling the world may, at times, raise the child's levels of stress. Andrew's mother gives a graphic account of her son's extreme experience of stress:

> If Andrew is 'overloaded' by an activity or has something he considers disagreeable happen to him, he will lock himself in his bedroom. This behaviour can last days or weeks, during which he will eat all his meals in his bedroom.

Some young children with autism experience fears and anxieties around household objects, e.g. vacuum cleaners, lawn mowers or unusual and idiosyncratic objects. The sources of stress for the child with autism are many. We need to be alert to possible sources of stress and to stressful states building up in the child so that we can, if possible, remove the trigger and take avoiding action. The following defusing techniques could be suggested:

- taking charge of the situation;
- diverting the child's attention;
- reducing the background stimulation;
- finding relaxing things for the child to do.

Very often physical activity, the use of calming music, a period with a favourite object, will help to de-stress the child. However, caution is necessary – to ensure that we do not inadvertently use the de-stressing activity as a reward/reinforcer.

Planned intervention

In the main, when young children with autism show behavioural difficulties which cause us as adults to experience worry, concern, anger, frustration and which indeed challenge us to widen our range of responses, they do not present single difficulties! Very often, a child who screams in rage and frustration also sleeps badly and may also have a very restricted diet. Another who sleeps and eats well may be 'non-compliant', withdrawing into rituals and routines. We are unlikely simply to need to change one behaviour. It is for this reason that a holistic view of the situation must be taken, and the overall needs of the child and the family be considered.

With reference to children's progress, Rogers (1996) writes: 'children with autism appear most able to benefit when intervention is begun very early, between ages two and four, making far more progress than do older children receiving the same interventions'. This definitely applies to behaviour. In the authors' experience, when children with autism are offered early autism-oriented educational intervention in appropriate settings on a daily basis, and where parents are involved, the incidence and severity of behavioural difficulties rapidly reduces. Children who are presenting behavioural difficulties may be in a very stressed state. An overall preventative approach should be employed as outlined earlier. However, it is often useful to be able to approach behavioural difficulties systematically – that is, to make a functional analysis of the presenting difficulties and then to make systematic alterations to the situations.

Identifying the nature of the behaviour

Challenging behaviour does not mean that the child is being deliberately awkward or defiant even though the behaviour can be accompanied by what may appear to be a 'knowing' look. Some behaviours become challenging as the child grows older and the cuteness of the three year old becomes a challenge in a 19 year old because the behaviour has not changed – unlike the size of the child. Context is also important: the young child who chooses not to wear clothes at home has difficulty accepting that he needs to wear clothes at school. The adults surrounding the child may also have different levels of tolerance regarding the acceptability of the behaviours.

In this context recognising a behaviour that is challenging is like looking through a kaleidoscope when one slight twist can make the view a myriad of pieces or a fascinating shape. This makes the need for understanding the nature of the behaviours and consistency of approach the prime requirement for all those who work with the child.

It is helpful to establish why certain behaviours occur – what's in it for the child? There is a range of reasons for any behaviour, positive or negative. Behaviours satisfy needs, may be a way of searching for stimulation, an enjoyable activity, a response to demands, a way of organising a seemingly disorganised world, a way of escaping stressful situations or a protest at any limits on free choice. They may be due to the situation, mood swings, the organic state, e.g. epilepsy, or an expression of pain. If it is possible to recognise the function of the behaviour then it may be feasible to offer an acceptable alternative if the behaviour causes a problem for the child.

Defining the problem

First it is necessary to define precisely the behaviour(s) under consideration. The description of the behaviour needs to be precise and phrased in observable and quantifiable terms, e.g. 'bites' or 'screams' rather than 'aggressive' or 'frustrated'.

There are many different forms for recording observations but most follow the classic model, the ABC.

Antecedent	Behaviour	Consequence
What happened immediately before the behaviour?	Describe the behaviour precisely, in clear terms.	What was the effect of the behaviour for the child?

For example a simple scenario may be:

Antecedent	Behaviour	Consequence
Toy was taken by another child.	Child screamed.	Adult returned the toy to the first child.

In this instance the behaviour communicates, 'I am upset' to the adult who returns the toy to the child. The child may learn that to scream means someone will do something for me. Zarkowska and Clements (1994) refine this model further, outlining the STAR approach in this way:

S represents *Settings*

T represents *Triggers*

A represents *Actions*

R represents *Results*

A simple example may be:

Settings	Triggers	Actions	Results
Large assembly hall Amongst 200 children and 10 adults Whole school act of worship Child in an aroused state Following known structure but understanding very little of what is said	Singing of hymn	Screaming Hitting out at the children around him Biting own hand	Removal from situation Engage in calming activity

In this case the information given gives a fuller picture of the incident. The child is in a situation that is causing him to become anxious. This is followed by singing which causes sensory overload. Consequently his frustration leads to hurting others and himself. He escapes from the situation and gains a positive preferred activity. The child may come to learn that this way of expressing frustration is the quickest way to escape from situations and get a preferred activity.

When records are kept following either of these models, over a period of time and in a variety of situations, it may become possible to answer such questions as:

What, precisely, is the behaviour we are dealing with?

How often is it occurring?

Is there a pattern to the triggers?

What is the consequence of the behaviour for the child?

Are we rewarding negative behaviours?

From this information, and in consultation with all who work with the child and the parents, the next questions need to be asked:

What can we do to reduce the frequency of the behaviours?

What can we do when the behaviours occur?

A word of warning at this stage – functional analysis of behaviour is not always simple. Human behaviour will always be determined by many factors and by different factors at different times. Sometimes there are multi-functions to the same behaviour. Children with autism often have their own idiosyncratic factors and responses. Observation, therefore, has an increased role to play.

At times it feels as though permission is needed to spend time observing a child, but if staff and parents are to feel confident they must get to know the child without feeling under pressure to be constantly intervening. Sometimes we think we know what is happening but in a busy situation there is always the possibility of people making assumptions about the reasons for behaviour based on their own view of the situation rather than seeing it from the child's point of view. We have to learn to think specifically rather than generally. Occasionally we need to unlearn our instinctive responses, and expand our professional training to become open-minded to ideas that help to meet specific needs which deviate from the expected. Careful detective work by the practitioner and parents using the 'Autism Lens' can suggest some useful hypotheses and a range of useful strategies.

Designing the intervention

It would not be possible to do justice here to the full range of Applied Behavioural Analysis techniques. The reader may wish to refer to Zarkowska and Clements (1994) for example, for a fuller explanation. Basic components of any programme to change behaviour and develop new skills will be:

- *Alter setting conditions first*
  Change the context and situation in which the behaviour occurs to eliminate 'triggers' if possible. 'Setting conditions' need to be viewed broadly and many aspects of the child's life considered, e.g. sleep patterns, diet, learning demands, environment, noise levels and physical activity.

- *Have a positive focus*
  There is likely to be greater progress under conditions which are positively reinforcing of desired behaviour instead of negative.
  Care must be taken to ensure that the positive reinforcers/rewards are actually rewarding for the child. Smiles and cuddles can have the opposite effect on the young child with autism to that intended. Stars and stickers may be meaningless to the child (see earlier paragraph 'Building in positives', p.85).
  Rewards may take the form of food, drinks, activities, toys, breaks, or 'obsessions'. They should be powerful and meaningful to the child. They should be used consistently and predictably at the outset of any change programme in order to be effective. Donnellan *et al.* (1988) describe a range of positive procedures for the practitioner who wishes to develop such strategies further.

- *Teach alternative skills*
  If the purpose and function of the behaviour can be identified by careful observation, then the child can be taught an alternative way of achieving these goals, for example using a symbol to indicate 'out' or 'more' instead of screaming (as with Emily following a PECS programme).

- *Use graded change techniques*
  A planned change in behaviour will usually entail careful analysis of the goal to be achieved, and the construction of a series of steps towards the eventual goal. The goal for Simon was to be able to be part of the hall assembly without screaming. The starting point was outside the hall. For Vivienne who refused to re-enter the classroom when the dinner smell put her off, and who stayed outside for two weeks, a careful programme of 'temptations' to cross the threshold was devised, including favoured aromatherapy smells, cooking activities, essential materials for tasks so that she gradually increased her time in the classroom.

- *Building in measurement and evaluation procedures*
  As in the initial recording of observation using ABC or STAR methods, any programme for behavioural change should be carefully recorded and monitored so that small changes are noted and the effectiveness of intervention may be measured.

- *Include collaboration with others*
  Joint planning between parents, teaching and support staff and other involved practitioners is important in tackling behavioural challenges. In devising a programme based on Applied Behavioural Analysis, the involvement of the Educational or Clinical Psychologist will be particularly helpful in planning and applying strategies. Early Years practitioners will also benefit from the Training Workshops in the Portage system if available. These cover techniques such as Reward/Reinforcement; Task Analysis; Shaping and Chaining.

Summary

A preventative approach is best and should include:

- understanding the sources of behavioural difficulties in autism;
- applying autism-specific approaches where appropriate;
- structuring the environment for prevention;
- providing a means of communication;
- tailoring social demands to the child's ability;
- differentiating learning;
- teaching play skills;
- teaching social skills;
- using clear rules;
- de-stressing;
- building in positives;
- allowing for interests/obsessions.

If a closer focus on specific behaviours is necessary, then systematic intervention based on a functional analysis, careful, informed, methodical observation and collection of data will be required:

- precisely defining the behaviour(s);
- identifying the purpose or function of the behaviour for the child;
- careful observation and recording of setting conditions, triggers for behaviours, actions or events, and their results;
- altering setting conditions to promote positive change;
- designing an intervention programme with a positive focus;
- ensuring rewards are meaningful and motivating for the child;
- teaching alternative skills;
- using graded change techniques.

7 Observation profile

Introduction

The purpose of the observation profile is to enhance the teacher's ability to assess the young child's progress in developing skills and understanding in those areas which are typically impaired in autism. In the authors' experience of training groups of support assistants and teachers from mainstream nursery and special schools, there is a reported dearth of readily accessible material examining the earliest stages of skill acquisition in these areas (although the P-level targets represent a recent attempt to redress this situation across the curriculum).

On the one hand, the profile should help to establish a baseline for skill acquisition and on the other, to demonstrate progress where intervention programmes have been introduced. The elements of the profile are thus organised in a broadly developmental sequence and are intended to indicate a sequential organisation of skill acquisition in developing goals. However, this is not to say that the young child with autism will progress in each area in an organised fashion! Skills in turn-taking may be more easily developed than those of imitation, for example. In developing imitation skills it may be that imitation of an action on an object – for example, dropping a brick into a cup – is more easily acquired than the social imitation of a gesture such as waving.

Use of the observation profile may assist practitioners in differentiating Early Learning Goals and in setting appropriate targets within the Individual Education Plan (IEP). Should more comprehensive analysis of skills be necessary, for example, in the area of communication, the use of assessment tools such as the Pragmatic Profile of Communication and the Pre-verbal Communication Schedule (see Chapter 2) may be helpful. Here, in best practice, the Early Years practitioner will be collaborating with the Speech and Language Therapist. In terms of more detailed analysis of early cognitive and play skills, use of the Uzgiris and Hunt based schedules for assessment and intervention would be complementary.

Use of the profile

Part 1: Word picture

One class teacher summarised a five year old girl in a mainstream class of 30 children as:

- an able child;
- she demands her own way;
- she can be noisy and disruptive;
- there are occasional violent outbursts;
- she does beautiful drawings of dinosaurs and insects.

This summary gives an overview of an able child with autism. However, it is necessary to fill out the details of the profile in order to find starting points for intervention.

Part 2: Observed behaviours

Children with autism share the same core difficulties, but each child displays these in an individual way.

The profile follows a broadly developmental sequence, but different children will make progress in different areas at different speeds. Each profile will be unique to that individual child, and will offer a snapshot of the child's skills.

For example (see Observation Profile that follows for key for N, I, D, F):

	N	I	D	F
Looks at adult who is talking to him			✔	
Follows adult gaze when adult is looking at something		✔		
Looks at object, then back at adult, when indicating, pointing to or requesting something	✔			

In this example, the developing use of gaze directed at the adult who is talking to him shows an awareness of the adult. The infrequent use of gaze to share the focus of attention suggests that the child is not yet aware of joint focus. Intervention that encourages the development of joint focus is indicated, e.g. Musical/Intensive Interaction activities (see Chapter 4).

Intervention planning

Once the goals have been identified in each skill area, they should be recorded on an Individual Education Plan (IEP), alongside suggested intervention strategies. These strategies should then inform curriculum differentiation across all areas of learning. For example:

Target	Strategies
The child will look at an adult who is talking to him	• identify attractive, eye-catching, noise producing items • introduce an item to the child, then hide it briefly, while looking towards where it is hidden • if necessary use the noise to attract the child's attention • wait until the child gives eye contact to reintroduce the toy with great gusto!

The Observation profile is not intended to be a diagnostic checklist. It is designed to give EarlyYears practitioners:

- information about the skills a child has already developed;
- starting points for intervention.

OBSERVATION PROFILE

Part 1. Give a brief word picture of the child in the Early Years setting, noting positive points as well as concerns.

Part 2.	**OBSERVED BEHAVIOURS**

Rate, using the following key: **N** = Not present   **I** = Infrequent
D = Developing   **F** = Fluent

A. Social Interaction

1. Spontaneous use of gaze	N	I	D	F
Looks at adult who is talking to him				
Follows adult gaze when adult is looking at something				
Looks at adult's face when trying to get his/her attention				
Looks at object, then back at adult, when indicating, pointing to or requesting something				
Looks back at adult when (s)he is playing chase with him				
Looks at adult to prompt the repeat of an action game or song				

2. Spontaneous maintenance of proximity				
Allows family members to kiss and hug him				
When upset, goes to family members for comfort				
Allows adult to physically interact in games of chase or 'rough and tumble'				
Allows physical interaction during action games or songs				
Allows adult to play alongside when engaged in an activity				
Allows adult to intervene/share in play				
Tolerates other children sitting nearby				
Allows other children to physically interact in games of chase				
Watches other children playing				
Tolerates other children playing alongside				
Tolerates other children intervening in his play				

3. Imitation				
Notices adult imitating him in action games and interactive play				
Responds to imitation of his actions with further repetition				
Initiates and pauses to allow imitation in social play				
Imitates simple gestures on cue, e.g. waving, clapping				
Imitates more complex gestures on cue, e.g. patting head, sticking tongue out				
Imitates actions with objects on cue, e.g. placing brick in cup, hitting drum with stick				
Imitates more complex actions, e.g. building brick tower				
Imitates simple facial expressions, e.g. smile, grimace				
4. Turn-taking				
Take turns, physically prompted, in simple ball game, e.g. rolling ball to and from adult				
Takes turns in simple ball games with adult/child				
Takes turns in table-top activity 1:1 with adult, e.g. building with bricks, placing pegs, matching pictures				
Takes turns in table-top activity with one other child				
Takes turns in table-top activity with more than one other child, e.g. Lotto game				
Takes turns in gross motor games, e.g. obstacle course				
Takes turns in circle time type activities				
Takes turns in more informally structured play, e.g. riding bikes, chasing games				
5. Initiating				
Uses sounds and gestures to attract adult attention				
Shows/offers object/activity to adult				
Shows/offers object/activity to another child				
Points to show interest in something				
Will take adult to object				
Will take adult's hand to object				
Waves 'bye-bye' spontaneously				

Greets familiar adults				
Indicates need for help by use of sound/gesture/picture				
Will approach adult to obtain food/toy, etc				
Will spontaneously approach adult when in need of help				
Will try to share interest or excitement with adult				
Will seek affection or comfort from adult other than family				
Will initiate a simple game with adult, e.g. pat-a-cake				
Will initiate a simple game with a child, e.g. chase				
Will give out snacks at break-time				

6. Emotional expression and understanding

Recognises a smile and can imitate adult's exaggerated demonstration of a smile				
Recognises a sad face and can imitate this				
Recognises an angry face and can imitate this				
Can discriminate these expressions on an adult face and can produce these expressions on demand				
Can recognise and match expressions in photographs				
Can recognise and match expressions in drawings				
Can match these simple expressions to contexts, e.g. matching 'smiling face' to picture of birthday presents				
Can respond to a smile with a smile				
Uses sad expression if upset				
Uses angry face if cross				
Developing understanding of other expressions, e.g. fear, surprise				

7. Development of self

Recognises mirror image/picture of self				
Knows own name – looks when called				
Knows own name – comes when called				
Knows own name – points to self when called				
Identifies/defends own possessions				

95

Shows preferences – for objects				
Shows preferences – for people				
Requests toys/activities/food he wants				
Makes choices when offered				

B. Communication

1. Understanding simple verbal and non-verbal approaches	N	I	D	F
Responds when his name is called				
Follows simple instructions given 1:1, e.g. 'come here', 'sit down'				
Follows a close point, e.g. at a picture in a book				
Follows a distance point, e.g. at object across the room				
Follows your gaze to an object				
Follows simple instructions in small groups				
Follows simple instructions in large group/class setting, e.g. 'jump', 'run', 'stand still'				
Could bring something on request from another room				
2. Strategies for meeting his needs				
Meets his needs independently, e.g. gets chair, climbs up to cupboard – rather than seeking help				
Stands near object and cries/screams until adult comes to reach it				
Requests object by taking adult to it or taking adult hand to it				
Requests object by pointing to it				
Requests object by pointing and looking back to adult				
Requests object by use of symbol/picture or photo				
Requests action by use of gesture				
Requests action by use of symbol/picture/photo				
Requests object/action using words				
Protests by crying/anger				
Protests by using sign/symbol/gesture or word				

3. Engaging in social interaction				
Can nod for 'yes'				
Can shake head for 'no'				
Uses greeting/gesture/sounds or words				
Waves and says 'bye-bye'				
Calls for attention				
Uses names to get attention, e.g. 'Mummy'				
Will take turns in familiar verbal routines, e.g. rhymes				
Will indicate desire for 'more' in familiar verbal routines				
Will fill in gaps in familiar verbal routines				
Will initiate familiar verbal routines with sounds/gestures /words				
4. Joint attention strategies				
Expresses interest in something, using sound/gesture				
Expresses interest in something using words				
Will point at something to express interest and shares this by looking back at you				
Uses expressive gesture, e.g. clapping				
C. Play and Imagination				
1. Manipulative/Exploratory	N	I	D	F
Plays with object using non-specific action on all objects, e.g. mouthing, waving, banging, shaking				
Examines novel toy/object				
Plays with objects using appropriate actions, e.g. bangs with hammer, shakes bell, throws ball, crumples paper				
2. Organising				
Relates toys/objects non-specifically, e.g. banging together, piling up				
Systematically combines objects, e.g. dumps out of/puts into containers; nests/stacks cups; stacks rings; strings beads				
3. Structured/Constructional				
Fitting items together by trial and error, e.g. Duplo bricks				

Completes simple formboards/puzzles/pegboard patterns				
Evidence of planning in problem solving				
4. Cause and Effect/Means to an End play				
Makes a toy work, e.g. presses button to make clown pop up; operates wind-up toy				
Uses object to obtain item, e.g. a stick to pull a toy within reach				
Climbs to reach toy				
Rolls ball to knock skittles down				
Searches for and finds objects during play				
5. Interactive				
Tolerates adult's presence during play				
Allows adult to intervene in play				
Will give object to adult during play, e.g. to ask for help				
Participates in rough and tumble play				
Allows adult to imitate his actions in play, e.g. in musical interaction				
Responds to play routines with enjoyment, e.g. peek-a-boo				
Responds with anticipation in play routines, e.g. 'I'm coming to get you!', and action rhymes, e.g. round the garden				
Indicates for game/routine to continue				
Initiates games/routines				
Will tolerate 'teasing' element in games/routines				
Will introduce 'teasing' element in games/routines				
Will take turns in games/play				
(See also Imitation and Turn-taking in Social Interaction section)				
6. Pretend play – functional				
Uses objects out of context and without situational cues, e.g. takes empty cup to mouth; holds brush to hair				
Will play functionally with objects, e.g. gives doll a 'drink' (in imitation); pushes car into garage (on instruction); builds network of blocks (on request/spontaneously)				

Will use miniature representational toys, e.g. Playmobil				
7. Pretend play – symbolic				
Uses toy/material as if it were something else, e.g. a stick for a spoon; a brush for a microphone				
Pretends to play with an absent object, e.g. feeds toys imaginary food				
In imitation, engages in linked sequence of actions, e.g. takes doll for a walk to park, goes on swings/slide/home to bed				
Does the above spontaneously				
Will make toy be something else, e.g. Mum/policeman				
Will make toy feel something, e.g. crying/angry				
Will make toy act upon imaginary objects				
8. Pretend play – fantasy				
Child will be someone/something else, e.g. dog/Dad/nurse/ Superman				
Does something to or with an imaginary object, e.g. strokes 'cat'				
Adopts and acts out a role, e.g. bus-driver/pilot/shop customer				
9. Pretend play – social				
Little contact with peers				
Watches peers playing				
Some parallel play				
Idiosyncratic approaches				
Brief exchanges				
Joint focus in play				
Role enactment				
Role play sustained				

Appendix 1: Diagnostic criteria for autism

1. From ICD 10 (World Health Organisation 1992)

A. Qualitative impairment in reciprocal social interaction, 3 from the following 5 areas:

1. Failure to use eye gaze, body posture, facial expression and gesture to regulate interaction adequately.
2. A failure to develop (in a manner appropriate to mental age, and despite ample opportunity) peer relationships that involve a mutual sharing of interests, activities and emotions.
3. Rarely seeking and using other people for comfort and affection at times of stress or distress and/or offering comfort and affection to others when they are showing distress or unhappiness.
4. A lack of shared enjoyment in terms of vicarious pleasures in other people's happiness and/or a spontaneous seeking to share their own enjoyment through joint involvement with others.
5. A lack of socio-emotional reciprocity, as shown by an impaired or deviant response to communicative behaviours.

B. Qualitative impairments in communication, 2 from the following 5 areas:

1. A delay in, or total lack of, spoken language that is not accompanied by an attempt to compensate through the use of gesture or mime as alternative modes of communication.
2. A relative failure to initiate or sustain conversational interchange (at whatever level of language skills is present) in which there is a reciprocal to and fro responsiveness to the communication of the other person.
3. Stereotyped and repetitive use of language and/or idiosyncratic use of words or phrases.
4. Abnormalities in pitch, stress, rate, rhythm, and intonation of speech.
5. A lack of varied spontaneous make-believe play, or, when young, social imitative play.

C. Restricted, repetitive, and stereotyped patterns of behaviour, interests and activities, 2 from the following 6 areas:

1. An encompassing preoccupation with stereotyped and restricted patterns of interest.
2. Specific attachments to unusual objects.
3. Apparently compulsive adherence to specific, non-functional routines or rituals.
4. Stereotyped and repetitive motor mannerisms that involve either hand/finger flapping or twisting or complex whole body movements.
5. Preoccupation with part-objects or non-functional elements of play materials (such as odour, the feel of their surface, or the noise/vibration that they generate).
6. Distress over changes in small, non-functional details of the environment.

D. Developmental abnormalities must be present in the first 3 years for the diagnosis to be made.

E. Clinical picture is not attributable to other varieties of pervasive developmental disorder; specific developmental disorder of receptive language with secondary socio-emotional problems; reactive attachment disorder or disinhibited attachment disorder; mental retardation with some associated emotional/behavioural disorder; schizophrenia of unusually early onset; and Rett syndrome.

Reprinted with permission from World Health Organisation (1992)
from the 10th revision of the *International Classification of Diseases (ICD–10)*
Geneva: World Health Organisation

2. From DSM IV (American Psychiatric Association 1994)

A. A total of six (or more) items from (1), (2) and (3), with at least two from (1), and one each from (2) and (3).

1. Qualitative impairment in social interaction, as manifested by at least two of the following:
a) Marked impairment in the use of multiple non-verbal behaviours such as eye to eye gaze, facial expression, body postures, and gestures to regulate social interaction.
b) Failure to develop peer relationships appropriate to developmental level.
c) A lack of spontaneous seeking to share enjoyment, interests, or achievements with other people (e.g. by a lack of showing, bringing, or pointing out objects of interest).
d) A lack of social or emotional reciprocity.

2. Qualitative impairments in communication as manifested by at least one of the following:

a) Delay in, or total lack of, the development of spoken language (not accompanied by an attempt to compensate through alternative modes of communication such as gesture or mime).
b) In individuals with adequate speech, marked impairment in the ability to initiate or sustain a conversation with others.
c) Stereotyped and repetitive use of language or idiosyncratic language.
d) Lack of varied, spontaneous make-believe play or social imitative play appropriate to developmental level.

3. Restricted, repetitive and stereotyped patterns of behaviour, interests, and activities, as manifested by at least one of the following:

a) Encompassing preoccupation with one or more stereotyped and restricted patterns of interest that is abnormal either in intensity or focus.
b) Apparently inflexible adherence to specific, non-functional routines or rituals.
c) Stereotyped and repetitive motor mannerisms (e.g. hand or finger flapping or twisting, or complex whole-body movements).
d) Persistent preoccupation with parts of objects.

B. Delays or abnormal functioning in at least one of the following areas (with onset prior to age 3 years):

a) Social interaction.
b) Language as used in social communication.
c) Symbolic or imaginative play.

C. The disturbance is not better accounted for by Rett disorder or Childhood Disintegrative Disorder.

Reprinted with permission from *The Diagnostic and Statistical Manual of Mental Disorders, Fourth Edition.* Copyright 1994 American Psychiatric Association

Appendix 2: Early Learning Goals: six areas of learning

(DfEE 2000)

1. Personal, Social and Emotional Development

By the end of the reception year, most children should:

- Continue to be interested, excited and motivated to learn
- Be confident to try new activities, initiate ideas and speak in a familiar group
- Maintain attention, concentrate and sit quietly when appropriate
- Respond to significant experiences, showing a range of feelings when appropriate
- Have a developing awareness of their own needs, views and feelings and be sensitive to the needs, views and feelings of others
- Have a developing respect for their own cultures and beliefs and those of other people
- Form good relationships with adults and peers
- Work as part of a group or class, taking turns and sharing fairly; understanding that there needs to be agreed values and codes of behaviour for groups of people, including adults and children, to work together harmoniously
- Understand what is right, what is wrong, and why
- Consider the consequences of their words and actions for themselves and others
- Dress and undress independently and manage their own personal hygiene
- Select and use activities and resources independently
- Understand that people have different needs, views, cultures and beliefs, that need to be treated with respect
- Understand that they can expect others to treat their needs, views, cultures and beliefs with respect

2. Communication, Language and Literacy

By the end of the reception year, most children should:

- Interact with others, negotiating plans and activities and taking turns in conversation
- Enjoy listening to and using spoken and written language, and readily turn to it in their play and learning
- Sustain attentive listening, responding to what they have heard by relevant comments, questions or actions
- Listen with enjoyment, and respond to stories, songs and other music, rhymes and poems and make up their own stories, songs rhymes and poems
- Extend their vocabulary, exploring the meanings and sounds of new words
- Speak clearly and audibly with confidence and control and show awareness of the listener, for example by their use of conventions such as greetings, 'please' and 'thank you'
- Use language to imagine and recreate roles and experiences
- Use talk to organise, sequence and clarify thinking, ideas, feelings and events
- Hear and say initial and final sounds in words, and short vowel sounds within words

- Link sounds to letters, naming and sounding the letters of the alphabet
- Use their phonic knowledge to write simple regular words and make phonetically plausible attempts at more complex words
- Explore and experiment with sounds, words and texts
- Retell narratives in the correct sequence, drawing on language patterns of stories
- Read a range of familiar and common words and simple sentences independently
- Know that print carries meaning and, in English, is read from left to right and top to bottom
- Show an understanding of the elements of stories, such as main character, sequence of events, and openings, and how information can be found in non-fiction texts to answer questions about where, who, why and how
- Use their phonic knowledge to write simple regular words and make phonetically plausible attempts at more complex words
- Attempt writing for different purposes, using features of different forms such as lists, stories and instructions
- Write their own names and other things such as labels and captions and begin to form simple sentences, sometimes using punctuation
- Use a pencil and hold it effectively to form recognisable letters, most of which are correctly formed

3. Mathematical Development

By the end of the reception year, most children should:

- Say and use number names in order in familiar contexts
- Count reliably up to 10 everyday objects
- Recognise numerals 1 to 9
- Use developing mathematical ideas and methods to solve practical problems
- In practical activities and discussion begin to use the vocabulary involved in adding and subtracting
- Use language such as 'more' or 'less' to compare two numbers
- Find one more or one less than a number from 1 to 10
- Begin to relate addition to combining two groups of objects and subtraction to 'taking away'
- Use language such as 'greater', 'smaller', heavier or 'lighter' to compare quantities
- Talk about, recognise and recreate simple patterns
- Use language such as 'circle' or 'bigger' to describe the shape and size of solids and flat shapes
- Use everyday words to describe position

4. Knowledge and Understanding of the World

By the end of the reception year, most children should:

- Investigate objects and materials by using all of their senses as appropriate
- Find out about, and identify, some features of living things, objects and events they observe
- Look closely at similarities, differences, patterns and change
- Ask questions about why things happen and how things work
- Build and construct with a wide range of objects, selecting appropriate resources, and adapting their work where necessary
- Select the tools and techniques they need to shape, assemble and join materials they are using
- Find out about and identify the uses of everyday technology and use information and communication technology and programmable toys to support their learning
- Find out about past and present events in their own lives, and in those of their families and other people they know
- Observe, find out about and identify features in the place they live and the natural world
- Find out about their environment and talk about those features they like and dislike
- Begin to know about their own cultures and beliefs and those of other people

5. Physical Development

By the end of the reception year, most children should:

- Move with confidence, imagination and safety
- Move with control and coordination
- Travel around, under, over and through balancing and climbing equipment
- Show awareness of space, of themselves and of others
- Recognise the importance of keeping healthy and those things that contribute to this
- Recognise the changes that happen to their bodies when they are active
- Use a range of small and large equipment
- Handle tools, objects, construction and malleable materials safely and with increasing control

6. Creative Development

By the end of the reception year, most children should:

- Explore colour, texture, shape, form and space in two or three dimensions
- Recognise how sounds can be changed, sing simple songs from memory, recognise repeated sounds and sound patterns and match movements to music
- Use their imagination in art and design, music, dance, imaginative and role play and stories
- Respond in a variety of ways to what they see, hear, smell, touch and feel
- Express and communicate their ideas, thoughts and feelings by using a widening range of materials, suitable tools, imaginative and role play, movement, designing and making, and a variety of songs and musical instruments

References

American Psychiatric Association (1994) *Diagnostic and Statistical Manual of Mental Disorders*, 4th edn (DSM IV). Washington DC: American Psychiatric Association.

Ashdown, J. (1993), in: Jordan, R. and Cornick, M. (1994) *Challenging Behaviour EDSEO2: Unit 5, Special Educational Needs of Pupils with Autism*. Birmingham: University of Birmingham.

August, G. J., Stewart, M. A. and Tsai, L. (1981) 'The incidence of psychological disabilities in the siblings of autistic children', *British Journal of Psychiatry* **138**, 416–422.

Baron-Cohen, S. (1987) 'Autism and symbolic play', *British Journal of Developmental Psychology* **5**(2), 139–148.

Baron-Cohen, S. (1995) *Mindblindness – An Essay on Autism and Theory of Mind*. Cambridge, Mass.: MIT Press.

Baron-Cohen, S. and Bolton, P. (1993) *Autism: the facts*. Oxford: Oxford University Press.

Baron-Cohen, S., Leslie, A. M. and Frith, U. (1985) 'Does the autistic child have a theory of mind?' *Cognition* **21**, 37–46.

Baron-Cohen, S. *et al.* (1992) 'Can autism be detected at 18 months? The needle, the haystack and the CHAT', *British Journal of Psychiatry* **161**, 839–43.

Baron-Cohen, S. *et al.* (1996) 'Psychological markers in the detection of autism in infancy in a large population', *British Journal of Psychiatry* **168**, 158–63.

Bettelheim, B. (1956) 'Childhood schizophrenia as a reaction to extreme situations', *Journal of Orthopsychiatry* **26**, 507–518.

Bishop, D.V.M. (1993) 'Autism executive functions and theory of the mind: a neurophysiological perspective', *Journal of Child Psychology and Psychiatry* **34**..

Beyer, J. and Gammeltoft, L. (2000) *Autism & Play*. London: Jessica Kingsley.

Bleuler, E. (1911) *Dementia praecox oder gruppe der schizophrenien* (J. Zinken translation 1950). New York: International University Press (originally published by Deutiche 1911).

Bolton, P. *et al.* (1994) 'A case-control family history study of autism'. *Journal of Child Psychology and Psychiatry* **35**, 877–90.

Bondy, A.S. and Frost, L.A. (1995) 'Educational approaches in preschool behaviour techniques in a public school setting', in Schopler, E. and Mesibor, G.B. *Learning and Cognition in Autism*. New York and London: Plenum Press.

Bondy, A.S. (1996) *The Pyramid Approach to Education*. Pyramid Educational Consultants.

Booth, T. (1983) 'Integrating special education: Introduction', in Booth, T. and Potts, P. *Integrating Special Education*. Oxford: Blackwell.

Booth. T. (1991) 'A perspective on inclusion from England', *Cambridge Journal of Education* **26**, 87–99.

Boucher, J. and Lewis, V. (1990) 'Guessing or creating? A reply to Baron-Cohen', *British Journal of Developmental Psychology* **8**, 205–09.

Carter, A. S. *et al.* (1998) 'The Vineland Adaptive Behaviour Scales: Supplementary norms for individuals with autism', *Journal of Autism and Developmental Disorders* **28**, 287–302.

Charlop-Christy, M.H. and Haymes L.A. (1998) 'Using objects of obsession as token reinforcers for children with autism', *Journal of Autism and Developmental Disorders*.

Christie, P. and Prevezer, W. (1998) *Interactive Play*. Nottingham: Early Years Diagnostic Centre (leaflet).

Christie, P. *et al.* (1992) 'An interactive approach to language and communication for non-speaking children', Lane, D. and Miller, A. (eds) *Child and Adolescent Therapy*. Milton Keynes: Open University Press.

Ciadella, P. and Mamelle, N. (1989) 'An epidemiological study of infantile autism in a French department (Rhone)', *Journal of Child Psychology and Psychiatry* **30**, 165–75.

Clarke, A. M. and Clarke, A. D. B. 'Formerly isolated children', in Clarke, A. M. and Clarke, A. D. B. (eds.) (1976) *Early Experience: Myth and Evidence*. London: Open Books.

Cumine, V., Leach, J. and Stevenson, G. (1998) *Asperger Syndrome – a practical guide for teachers*. London: David Fulton Publishers.

Department for Education and Employment (1999) *Early Learning Goals*. London: Qualifications and Curriculum Authority.

Department for Education and Employment (2000) *Curriculum Guidance for the Foundation Stage*. London: Qualifications and Curriculum Authority.

Dewart, H. and Summers, S. (1988) *The Pragmatic Profile of Early Communication Skills*. Windsor: NFER Nelson.

Di Lavore, P. C., Lord, C. and Rutter, M. (1995) 'The pre-linguistic autism diagnostic observation schedule', *Journal of Autism and Developmental Disorders* **25**, 355–379.

Donnellan, A. M. *et al.* (1988) *Progress without punishment – Effective approaches for learners with behaviour problems*. New York: Teachers' College Press.

Ehlers, S. and Gillberg, C. (1993) 'The epidemiology of Asperger syndrome – a total population study', *Journal of Child Psychology and Psychiatry* **34**, 1327–50.

Filipek, P.A. *et al.* (1999) 'The screening and diagnosis of autistic spectrum disorders', *Journal of Autism and Developmental Disorders* **29**(6), 439–84.

Folstein, S. and Rutter, M. (1977) 'Infantile autism: a genetic of 21 twin pairs', *Journal of Child Psychology and Psychiatry* **18**, 297–321.

Frith, U. (1989) *Autism: Explaining the Enigma*. Oxford: Blackwell.

Frith, U. (1991) *Autism and Asperger syndrome*. Cambridge: Cambridge University Press.

Frith, U., Soares, I. and Wing, L. (1993) 'Research into the earliest detectable signs of autism: what parents say' *Communication* **27**(3), 17–18.

Frost, L. A. and Bondy, A. S. (1994) *PECS: The Picture Communication System – Training Manual*. Cherry Hill, N J: Pyramid Educational Consultants.

Gillberg, C. and Coleman, C. (1992) *The Biology of the Autistic Syndromes*. London: MacKeith.

Gillberg, C. and Forsell, C. (1984) 'Childhood psychosis and neurofibromatosis – more than just a coincidence?' *Journal of Autism and Developmental Disorders* **14**, 1–8.

Gillberg, I. C., Gillberg, C. and Ahlsen, G. (1994) 'Autistic behaviour and attention deficits in tuberous sclerosis : a population based study', *Developmental Medicine and Child Neurology* **36**, 50–56.

Gillberg, C., Steffenburg, S. and Schaumann, H. (1991) 'Autism: Epidemiology – is autism more common now than 10 years ago?', *British Journal of Psychiatry* **158**, 403–409.

Grandin, T. (1995) 'How people with autism think', in Schopler, E. and Mesibov, G.B. (eds) *Learning and Cognition in Autism*. New York: Plenum Press.

Grandin, T. and Scariano, M. (1986) *Emergence labelled autistic*. Tunbridge Wells: Costello.

Gray, C. (1997) *Social Stories and Comic Strip Conversations*. Bicester, Oxon: Winslow Press.

Gray, C. (2000) Unpublished personal communication.

Guralnick, M. J. (1997) *The Effectiveness of Early Intervention*. Baltimore: Brookes Publishing.

Happe, F. (1994) *Autism : An introduction to psychological theory*. London: UCL Press.

Harris, P. (1993) 'Pretending and planning', in Baron-Cohen, S., Tager-Flusberg, H. and Cohen, D. J. (eds) *Understanding other minds – Perspectives from autism*. Oxford: Oxford University Press.

Helps, S. *et al.* (1998) 'Autism: the teacher's view', *Autism Journal* **3**(2), 287–298.

Hewett, D. and Nind, M. (eds) (1998) *Interaction in Action*. London: David Fulton Publishers.

Hobson, R. P. (1993) *Autism and the development of mind*. Hove, East Sussex: Laurence Erlbaum Associates.

Howlin, P. and Rutter, M. (1987) *Treatment of Autistic Children*. Chichester: John Wiley.

Howlin, P. and Moore, A. (1997) 'Diagnosis in autism', *Autism, the International Journal of Research and Practice* **2**, 135–62.

Humphrey, N. (1984) *Consciousness Regained*. Oxford: Oxford University Press.

Jarrold, C., Boucher, J. and Smith, P. K. (1996) 'Generating deficits in pretend play in autism', *British Journal of Developmental Psychology* **14**, 275–300.

Jordan, R.R. (1991). Two Conflicting Therapies? 'The Option Method and Behaviourism as Treatments for the Fundamental Difficulties of Autism: Therapeutic Approach to Autism: Research and Practice' Collected Papers from the conference organised by *Autism Research Unit* which is supported by the National Autistic Society and Sunderland Polytechnic.

Jordan, R. (1999) *Autistic Spectrum Disorders*. London: David Fulton Publishers.

Jordan, R. and Powell, S. (1995) *Understanding and Teaching Children with Autism*. Chichester: John Wiley.

Kanner, L. (1943) 'Autistic disturbances of affective contact', *Nervous Child* **2**, 217–50.

Kiernan, C. C. and Reid, B. (1987) *Pre-verbal Communication Schedule*. Slough: NFER Nelson.

Le Couteur, A. *et al.* (1989) 'Autism Diagnostic Interview : A standardised investigation-based instrument', *Journal of Autism and Developmental Disorders* **19**, 363–87.

Le Couteur, A. *et al.* (1996) 'A broader phenotype of autism: The clinical spectrum in twins', *Journal of Autism and Developmental Disorders* **24**, 155–76.

Lewis, R., Prevezer, W. and Spencer, R. (1996) *Musical Interaction: An Introduction*, Ravenshead, Nottinghamshire : Information Service, Early Years Centre.

Lewis, V. and Boucher, J. (1988) 'Spontaneous, instructed and elicited play in relatively able autistic children', *British Journal of Developmental Psychology* **6**(4), 325–39.

Lister-Brooke, S. and Bowler, D. (1992) 'Autism by another name? Semantic and pragmatic impairments in children', *Journal of Autism and Developmental Disorders* **22**, 61–82.

Lord, C. (1991) 'Follow up of 2 year olds referred for possible autism'. Paper presented at the biennial meeting of the Society for Research in Child Development, Seattle.

Lord, C. (1995) 'Follow-up of two-year-olds referred for possible Autism', *Journal of Child Psychology and Psychiatry* **36**(8).

Lord, C. and Schopler, E. (1987) 'Neurobiological implications of sex differences in autism', in Schopler, E. and Mesibov, G. M. (eds) *Neurobiological Issues in Autism*. New York: Plenum Press.

Lord, C. *et al.* (1989) 'Autism Diagnostic Observation Schedule : A standardised observation of communicative and social behaviour', *Journal of Autism and Developmental Disorders* **19**, 185–212.

Lotter, V. (1966) 'Epidemiology of autistic conditions in young children: prevalence', *Social Psychiatry* **1**, 124–37.

Lovaas O.I. (1987) Behavioural treatment and normal educational and intellectual functioning in young autistic children *Journal of Consulting and Clinical Psychology* **55** 3–9.

Meltzoff, A. and Gopnik, A. (1993) 'The role of imitation in understanding persons and developing a theory of mind', in Baron-Cohen, S. *et al.* (eds.) *Understanding Other Minds: Perspectives from Autism*. Oxford: Oxford University Press.

Neaum, S. and Tallack, J. (1997) *Good Practice in Implementing the Pre-school Curriculum*. London: Nelson Thornes.

Newson, E. (1979) 'Play-based observation for assessment of the whole child', in Newson, E. & Newson, J. *Toys and Playthings in Development and Remediation*. London: Penguin/Allen & Unwin.

Newson, E. (1993) 'Play based assessment in the special needs classroom', in Harris, J. (ed.) *Innovations in Educating Children with Severe Learning Difficulties*. Chorley: Lisieux Hall.

Nind, M. and Hewett, D. (1994) *Access to Communication*. London: David Fulton Publishers.

Olsson, I., Steffenburg, S. and Gillberg, C. (1988) 'Epilepsy in autism and autistic-like conditions – a population based study', *Archives of Neurology* **45**, 666–8.

Osterling, J. and Dawson, G. (1994) 'Early recognition of children with autism: a study of first birthday home videotapes', *Journal of Autism and Developmental Disorders* **24**, 247–59.

Ozonoff, S. (1995) 'Executive functions in autism', in Schopler, E. and Mesibov, G. B. (eds) *Learning and Cognition in Autism*. New York: Plenum Press.

Ozonoff, S., Pennington, S. J. and Rogers, B. F. (1991) 'Executive function deficits in high functioning autistic children: relationship to theory of mind', *Journal of Child Psychology & Psychiatry* **32**, 1081–106.

Peacock, G., Forrest, A. and Mills, R. (1996) *Autism – The invisible children*. London: National Autistic Society.

Powell, S. and Jordan, R. (1993) 'Being subjective about autistic thinking and learning to learn', *Educational Psychology* **13**, 359–70.

Powell, S. and Jordan, R. (1997) *Autism and Learning*. London: David Fulton Publishers.

Powers, S. (1992) in Freeman, R. J. (1997) *Journal of Autism and Developmental Disorders*. December.

Prevezer, W. (1990) Strategies for tuning into Autism *Therapy Weekly* **4**

Rapin, I. and Allen, A. (1983) 'Developmental language disorders: nosological considerations', in Kirk, V. (ed.) *Neuropsychology of Language, Reading and Spelling*. London: Academic Press.

Reichelt, K. L. *et al.* (1986) Childhood Autism. A complex disorder' *Biological Psychology* **21**, 1279–1290.

Rimland, B. (1990) 'Sound sensitivity in Autism'. *Autism Research Review International* **4**

Rogers, S. J. (1996) 'Brief report: Early Intervention in Autism', *Journal of Autism and Developmental Disorders* **26**(2), 243–6.

Roid, G. and Miller, L. (1997) *Leiter International Performance Scales – Revised*. Illinois: Stoelting.

Rossetti, L. M. (1996) *Communication Intervention: Birth to three*. San Diego: Singular Publishing.

Russell, J., Saltmarsh, R. and Hill, E. (1999) 'What do executive factors contribute to the failure on false belief tasks by children with autism?', *Journal of Child Psychology and Psychiatry* **40**(6), 859–68.

Rutter, M. (1970) 'Autistic children: Infancy to adulthood', *Seminars in Psychiatry* **2**, 435–50.

Rutter, M. (1978) 'Diagnosis and definition of childhood autism', *Journal of Autism and Childhood Schizophrenia* **8**, 138–61.

Rutter, M. (1979) 'Language, cognition and autism', in Katzman, R. (ed.) *Congenital and Acquired Cognitive Disorders*. New York: Rarcus Press.

Schopler, E. (1984) *Psychoeducational Profile (PEP)* Austin, Texas: Pro-Ed.

Schopler, E. (1989) 'Principles for directing both education, treatment and research', in Gillberg, C. (ed.) *Diagnosis and Treatment in Autism*. New York: Plenum Press.

Schopler, E., Reichler, R. and Rochen–Renner, B. (1988) *The Childhood Autism Rating Scale (CARS)*. Los Angeles: Western Psychological Services.

Schopler, E. *et al.* (1990) Psychoeducational profile – Revised (PEP-R). Austin, Texas: Pro-Ed.

Schopler, E. and Mesibor, G.B. (1995) *Learning and Cognition in Autism*. London: Plenum Press.

Shah, A. and Frith, U. (1993) 'Why do autistic individuals show superior performance on the block design task?', *Journal of Child Psychology and Psychiatry* **34**, 1351–64.

Shattock, P. (1990) 'Some Implicaitons of basic physiological research for the behaviour and treatment of people with autism.' Proceedings from '*Experimental Psychology & Autistic Syndromes*' Durham National Autistic Society. 275–285.Shattock, P. (1998) 'Diet', *Communication*, Summer.

Sherratt, D. (1999) *The Importance of Play – Good Autism Practice*. Birmingham: University of Birmingham.

Smalley, S. L., Asarnov, R. F. and Spence, A. (1988) 'Autism and genetics: a decade of Research', *Archives of General Psychiatry* **45**, 953–61.

Sparrow, S. S., Balla, D. A. and Cicchetti, D. V. (1984) *Vineland Adaptive Behaviour Scales* (Expanded edition). Circle Pines: American Guidance Service.

Steffenburg, S. and Gillberg, C. (1990) 'The etiology of autism', in Gillberg, C. (ed.) *Autism Diagnosis and Treatment*. New York: Plenum Press.

Stehli, A. (1992) *The Sound of a Miracle: a Child's Triumph over Autism* . USA: Fourth Estate.

Trevarthen, C. *et al.* (1996) *Children with Autism: diagnosis and interventions to meet their needs*. London: Jessica Kingsley.

van Bourgondien, M. E. (1993) 'Behaviour management in the pre-school years', in Schopler, E. and van Bourgondien, M. E. *Pre-school Issues in Autism*. New York: Plenum Press.

Vygotsky, L.S. (1966) 'Play and its role in the mental development of the child', *Soviet Psychology* **12** (original work published in 1933).

Vygotsky, L. S. (1978) *Mind in Society: The development of higher psychological processes*. Cambridge, Mass: Harvard University Press.

Warnock Report (1978) *Special Educational Needs*. London: HMSO.

Wechsler, D. (1991) *Wechsler Intelligence Scale for Children (WISC)*. New York: Harcourt Brace Jovanovitch.

Whiteley, P. *et al.* (1999) 'A gluten-free diet as an intervention for autism and associated spectrum disorders: preliminary findings', *Autism, the International Journal of Research and Practice* **3**(1), 45–66.

Williams, D. (1998) *Like Colour to the Blind*. London: Jessica Kingsley.

Williams, E., Costall, A. and Reddy, V. (1999) 'Children with Autism experience problems with both objects and people', *Journal of Autism and Developmental Disorders* **29**.

Wing, L. (1988) 'The continuum of autistic disorders', in Schopler, E. and Mesibov, G. M. (eds) *Diagnosis and Assessment in Autism*. New York: Plenum Press.

Wing, L. (1996) *The Autistic Spectrum: A guide for parents and professionals*. London: Constable.

Wing, L. (1997) 'The autistic spectrum', *Lancet* **350**, 1761–6.

Wing, L. and Gould, J. (1979) 'Severe impairments of social interaction and associated abnormalities in children: epidemiology and classification', *Journal of Autism and Developmental Disorders* **9**, 11–29.

Wolfberg, P. J. (1999) *Play and Imagination in Children with Autism*. New York: Teachers' College Press.

World Health Organisation (1992) *International Statistical Classification of Diseases and Related Health Problems, 10th edition (ICD 10)*. Geneva: World Health Organisation.

Zarkowska, E. and Clements, J. (1994) *Problem Behaviour and People with Severe Learning Disabilities*. London: Chapman and Hall.

Index